GREEN

# Stain Busters

## ABOUT THE AUTHOR

Alisa Mayne was raised completely self sufficient in Victoria by her parents Peter and Cynthia Mayne, and has written two books with her mother on the subjects of getting back to basics in the kitchen.

Cynthia was considered an expert in the field of budget and natural cooking and cleaning and together Cynthia and Alisa have given many media and library talks on the subject. Sadly Cynthia passed away after they wrote this book but not before teaching her daughter all she knew from her 40 years experience.

Alisa runs her own food business and picnic wedding catering service, which specialises in food made from scratch. She created a unique picnic restaurant that only takes bookings for trees and moves to different scenic locations and farms throughout the year. Her travelling restaurant is the only one of its kind in the world, where guests enjoy handmade local food free from any preservatives or additives, served in vintage timber apple crates and enjoyed outdoors. She lives in the Sunshine Coast hinterland with her husband Pete and is an advocate for natural, simple healthy lifestyles and supporting local producers.

Alisa's previous books 'how to feed your family for $75 a week' and 'how to feed yourself for $35 a week' are available online by contacting feedyourfamilybooks@gmail.com. Full details on her business 'Love My Food' can be found at www.lovemyfood.net.

## DEDICATION

This book was co-written by and dedicated to my wonderful Mumma, Cynthia Mayne. Mumma, together we wrote books based on what you taught us, to help people realise that life is wonderful no matter what your budget, and your wise words have helped so many. Everything I have learnt I learnt from you. Your unconditional love and compassion was truly unique. Your cheeky enthusiasm for life was infectious and your never ending quest to help people was inspiring. You gave so much and lived life to the absolute fullest. There will never be another like you and you are sorely missed by us all. Rest in Peace beautiful Mumma, we are so proud of you. xxoo

Published by:
Wilkinson Publishing Pty Ltd
ACN 006 042 173
Level 4, 2 Collins St Melbourne, Victoria, Australia 3000
Ph: +61 3 9654 5446
www.wilkinsonpublishing.com.au

National Library of Australia Cataloguing-in-Publication entry

| | |
|---|---|
| Creator: | Mayne, Alisa, author. |
| Title: | Stain busters : the environmentally safe cleaning guide / Alisa Mayne. |
| ISBN | 9781925265941 (paperback) |
| Series: | WP smart series. |
| Subjects: | Spotting (Cleaning)--Handbooks, manuals, etc. |
| | House cleaning--Handbooks, manuals, etc. |
| | Green products. |
| Dewey Number: | 648.5 |
| Layout Design: | Tango Media Pty Ltd |
| Cover Design: | Tango Media Pty Ltd |

Additional research and writing by
Connie Hatzikalimnios

Photos and illustrations by agreement with international agencies, photographers and illustrators including Getty Images and iStock.

# CONTENTS

# INTRODUCTION

**WELCOME TO THE** wonderful world of cleaning and the joy of working with ingredients that bubble and clean, glide and gleam as you work your way through the household chores. Cleaning is a fascinating study of chemical action and reaction – from active to inactive, from dirty to clean. It's also a great way to study nature's amazing ability to effect change from the simplest of ingredients.

Just as we are becoming more aware of the importance of what we put into our bodies through a healthy diet, so too should we be conscious of what products and chemicals we use around the home.

How many times have you picked up a commercial cleaner and struggled to decipher let alone pronounce the long list of complicated ingredients? What if I told you that you can achieve similar, if not better, results for a fraction of the commercial prices while using safe and natural ingredients found in the common home? Have I got your attention?

In this book you'll find clever, cost-effective, environmentally friendly recipes for keeping every inch of your home spotless using everyday ingredients such as lemons, vinegar and bicarb soda to beat the commercial products at their game!

With tips on cleaning up stubborn food, drink and grease stains, and advice on how to keep everything from your kitchen sink to your bathroom tiles looking as clean as the day they were installed, this is the must-have guide to home cleaning and taking control of your cleaning budget and environmental impact.

Don't keep all the fun for yourself though; involve the children in your home cleaning revolution and you'll be giving them a subtle lesson in stepping aside from the commercial push to buy the latest, and supposedly greatest, to the gentle world of being in control of your own environment. I've also included a few games for the children as a bonus, showing them the fun science behind many of the cleaning recipes using vinegar and bicarb soda.

I hope you enjoy the book, I certainly had fun putting everything together, and the bonus for me was I ended up with the cleanest home ever; the kitchen bench glows, the bathroom gleams, the floors shine and the windows glisten. And all for less than the price of a cup of coffee!

# THE SECRET THE BIG COMPANIES DON'T WANT US TO KNOW

**ALTHOUGH** cleaning products aren't a major part of the household budget, they are expensive and the cost of creams, polishes, powders and spray-on cleaners can be replaced with simple homemade products that work just as well for a fraction of the cost.

The cleaning products aisle is interesting to say the least – the variety is enormous and the scents overwhelming. There are so many things to do 'this' and 'that' to anything around your house it's hard to imagine that all we need to clean our homes is a few simple ingredients that can be bought in bulk for very little outlay.

Companies use the same base formula for many products. I know this because my mother used to supply a major super-market with a range of cleaners. Don't be fooled by the array of products on sale, most have the same active ingredient and often all that changes is the perfume, colouring and the ratio of active ingredient to water.

A base formula for a kitchen counter spray is often the same as an engine degreaser, they are just mixed in different ratios then presented in eye catching packaging giving the subtle message that we need to buy different products for each job. There's nothing wrong with these marketing games, after all "that's business". Cash in on the secrets of the big companies and make your home the centre for the business of saving money, reducing landfill and protecting our precious environment.

# SIMPLE CHANGES

**THEY SAY CHANGE** is not easy, especially in a world where time is short and stress levels high. Habit keeps us in a rut where we can be tempted to reach out for familiar items without giving thought to what we are really doing. Because change can be hard, especially in a busy household, try leaving notes around the house to avoid falling into old habits. Eventually new habits form and the notes can be discarded.

To make the transition from consumerism to homemade products stress free, put aside a place to store your basic ingredients; somewhere easy to get to. Then set about changing labels on the cleaning products you already have. The trick is to make the transition process as easy as possible and then you won't fall back into old habits.

Work with the principle of *waste not want not* and finish the commercial products you already have in your cupboard. Cover the commercial labels with your home formulae label and when the bottle is empty you're ready to move into action.

If you're lucky enough to still have the pitter-patter of tiny (or not so tiny) feet around the house ask the kids to liven the labels up with drawings and bright colours. Maybe they would like to choose names for each product. Getting them involved is a great way to help them understand the subtle methods of marketing because nothing teaches more than 'doing'.

Involving children in any activity will be more effective and it won't be long before your cupboards will outshine any supermarket aisle for colour and vibrancy.

## Prepare Ahead

When you prepare your mixture ahead of time it does make it easier to avoid being tempted to reach for that quick fix – the commercial alternative – and because, like commercial products, our homemade products will often have the some common active ingredients, it's a logical step to make bulk batches, store, then dilute as needed.

Being prepared also saves you the bother of having to remember all the various uses and formulations in your head; label the container according to the purpose, include the formula for easy refilling and your work is done.

Squeeze-top and spray-nozzle plastic bottles make good containers for liquids; a big plastic salt shaker with large holes in the top makes a good container for powders, and wide mouthed plastic containers with screw lids are ideal for gumption or paste cleaners.

It won't be long before commercial products are well and truly a thing of the past.

# A BIT ON THE SIDE

SOME INGREDIENTS are best purchased in bulk, which means you'll have enough raw ingredients to last a very long time. This isn't necessarily a bad thing because the ingredients won't go off if stored properly and buying in bulk offers another possibility – a source of some money on the side. Round up a few busy friends and sell them your surplus at a minimal cost.

Bartering with products in a suburban situation may not be convenient but bartering with money, the most common transaction is fail-proof and here is where your surplus product can make you extra cash, saving your friends money at the same time. It's also a chance for the children to design customised labels and spread their talents further afield.

## It Makes Sense and Cents

We know people find it hard to imagine cleaning the kitchen counter for 1 cent, or making an all purpose spray cleaner for 3 cents, but that's about all the raw ingredients in those highly priced products on the supermarket shelves cost the manufacturer. The rest is all in marketing, labelling, packaging, freight and presentation.

Now that you are becoming your own marketing company, labelling and packaging company, freight carrier and retailer, you're first in line to pick up the savings.

If you're keen on delicate perfumes and essential oils we encourage you to experiment. You may even come up with something totally new.

*A word of warning before you get started on your own recipes – some combinations can be toxic. Avoid mixing ammonia and bicarb soda; this mixture releases toxic gas (it's always advisable to avoid inhaling ammonia under any circumstances).*

# SOME OF THE THINGS **YOU WILL NEED** TO GET STARTED

**YOU'LL SAVE HEAPS** if you buy in bulk from a produce store, you can save up to 80% and because these ingredients don't expire there's no problem with waste.

But first a little more information about the ingredients, what they are, where they come from and what wonderful things they do.

+ **Pure soap**
+ **Bicarbonate of soda**
+ **Sodium per-carbonate**
+ **Citric acid**
+ **White vinegar**
+ Borax
+ **Washing soda**
+ Cloudy ammonia
+ **Salt (bulk)**
+ Tea tree or eucalyptus oil
+ **Lemon juice (fresh)**

If you buy in bulk from a produce store, you can save up to 80%.

# Pure soap

Pure Sunlight soap is the best to work with but is not always readily available so look for a good quality laundry soap bar.

I make a bulk mixture of liquid soap from 1 bar of soap grated and dissolved in 10 litres of water, and store it in an old 10L plastic water container with a tap so it's easy to decant. This ratio works for me but experiment with what suits your climate; in a cold climate the mixture will thicken on cold days but if you live in a hot climate you can probably reduce the water and use a more con-centrated liquid. Either way you'll find your perfect mix after some experiments.

Grating can be a bit of a bore, especially if the bar of soap has been wet or you have wet hands; the soap slips and slides all over the place. If you find grating a chore try cutting the soap into little pieces with a large knife. It will come away in long shards that may take a bit longer to dissolve but is much faster than grating.

Make sure you clean the bench and grater or knife as soon as you've finished. Your family won't share your sense of humour if you laugh when they pick up what they think are left over gratings of cheese from the bench to nibble as they pass by!

# TO MAKE THE
# BULK LIQUID SOAP

▶Dissolve 1 bar of grated soap in 2 litres of water over a medium heat.

▶Let the mixture cool.

▶Pour the dissolved liquid into a 10 litre container (an old water container is perfect) then top with a further 8 litres of cold water. This will give you a total of around 10 litres of liquid soap.

▶If you put the container with the dissolved soap liquid under the tap to top it up you'll find that bubbles will quickly take over. Avoid creating a container full of bubbles by pouring the water in at an angle, as you would pour a beer, or add the water first then top up with the concentrated soap liquid. It's a bit like life – slow and steady is the best pace.

If you don't have an empty 10L container use 5 x 2L milk containers and use the same ratio; ¼ melted soap to ¾ cold water. The container is not important, as long as it's convenient for you to handle.

The added water keeps the mixture liquid. A strong mixture will solidify when it's cold, which isn't particularly a problem because you can reheat it easily. Adding the extra cold water just saves you the bother.

# Bicarbonate of soda

Grandma's kitchen was never without it.

Chemically known as sodium bicarbonate, it's a soda ash which occurs naturally. It is refined to produce a pure safe product with many uses. It is not a chemical compound.

The beauty of bicarb, as it's commonly referred to, is that it helps regulate pH and balance acidity or alkalinity, which is why it's used a lot in food production. It's a neutraliser – the ultimate mediator with no end of uses including detergents, soakers, hair products and as an odour absorber. It's even used to make our bread rise.

The bicarb soda you use in your fridge, freezer or cupboard to eliminate odours can be used to clean your counters, floors and in your laundry. It's also a superb toothpaste and tooth whitener.

If kept for long periods or exposed to moisture it tends to 'clump', just tap with a wooden spoon to break up any lumps. A simple way of keeping it in easy-flow mode is to store bicarb in the fridge, because refrigerators dry things out.

Bicarb has so many uses we could do a book on that subject alone but all you need to know is that it's very safe for you, your family, your wallet and the environment. And it's fun to play with, as you'll see later.

# Sodium per-carbonate

Sodium per-carbonate is basically a solid form of hydrogen peroxide and is an environmentally safe whitening agent and deodoriser used in commercial laundry and cleaning products.

Stock can be obtained from chemical suppliers, pool supply companies and from the internet.

Sodium per-carbonate is not cheap but it is so powerful that you literally need only a pinch to get the desired boost.

# Citric acid

Citric acid is a dry powder or crystal, and is often called "sour salt". It is used extensively in cosmetics, foods and soft drinks, a host of industrial applications, and has proven to be an excellent de-greaser and cleaning agent.

Citric binds metals, cleans scale, adds bubbles to soft drinks, holds colour in jams, is used in ice cream as an emulsifying agent and in bath bombs and effervescent tablets – it is a most versatile product.

It is sold in supermarkets in small containers and can also be bought in larger quantities (and cheaper) from the chemist or wholesale distributors.

# Borax

Borax, or sodium borate as it's also known, is another fantastic natural substance. It was first discovered over 4,000 years ago and is a naturally occurring alkaline mineral.

Borax is usually found in the cleaning aisle of your supermarket (probably on the bottom shelf) and would be near the laundry powders and soaps, but the cheapest way is to buy it in bulk from hardware or produce stores.

The most common use for borax is as a laundry booster, it is fantastic if you live in an area with hard water because it's a superb water softener and leaves your clothes clean and bright.

Borax has been used for many generations for a range of things from disinfecting and deodorising to preserving cut flowers and even repelling bugs.

Borax has no toxic fumes and is safe for the environment, but take note that it can irritate the skin and should never be ingested.

Borax is a fantastic cleaning agent and as you will see in the recipes on the pages ahead, the good well outweighs the bad.

# Vinegar

Vinegar originated in France thousands of years ago from a barrel of wine that had gone bad; the French word 'vinaigre' literally translating to 'sour wine'.

The history of vinegar goes back 10,000 years when it was used by everyone; kings, queens and peasants. It's a testament to the value of vinegar in the lives of our ancestors that it was the only product shared across all classes of society, rich and poor alike.

There are thousands of uses for vinegar to back the claim that it is 'the product that can do anything'.

Getting technical; vinegar is an acidic liquid processed from the fermentation of ethanol in a process that yields acetic acid (ethanoic acid). The concentration ranges from 4% to 8% by volume when it's table vinegar (usually around 5%) and up to 18% for other uses.

Natural vinegars also contain small amounts of tartaric acid, citric acid and other acids and if you're lucky enough to get hold of a table vinegar with the 'mother' you know you've got the best on offer. Vinegar is a live product; the mother is the sediment formed in the processing and appears as a semi solid mass in top quality vinegars - a great internal cleanser.

But back to the household variety of cleanser – white vinegar. It's cheap, easy to use, totally natural and totally safe.

# Lemon juice

Most common commercial cleaning products contain lemon (or a chemically enhanced substitute) because the fresh scent of lemons makes people think of cleanliness, and because the citric acid contained in lemons is a strong cleaning agent. It's also a natural antiseptic.

The best lemons to use are those that have smooth oily skins and are heavy for their size (meaning plenty of juice). They should be bright yellow (ripe) with no green tinges (not ripe yet). Meyer lemons are the most alkaline and have very little pectin, while Lisbon or Eureka varieties are more acidic with plenty of pectin, which is why they are preferred for jam making.

Lemons keep well at room temperature but keep better in a cool, dry environment, and lemon zest (peel) can be frozen for months.

Depending on where you live lemon trees can be grown fairly easily. If you don't have a tree of your own keep an eye out for a tree in someone else's backyard and come to an arrangement to relieve the owner of the unwanted crop; maybe share your home-made cleaning products with them, or maybe they would just appreciate the surplus fruit being collected rather than rotting on the ground.

To get the most amount of juice the lemon should be at room temperature. Use the palm of your hand to roll the lemon on a hard surface to help improve juice yields.

If you only need a small amount of juice and don't want to waste a whole lemon pierce the end of the lemon with a fork, squeeze out the amount of juice needed, cover the holes with tape and then store in the fridge.

Or you could cut a small sliver of rind and, when you've taken what juice you need, simply replace the rind back over the hole. It will re-seal itself and be ready for next time.

Isn't nature great – a no fuss, superbly fashioned, environmentally friendly container at your fingertips!

Lemons are another of nature's magic products that smell good, store well, are environmentally friendly and don't cost the earth.

# Salt

Salt is a mineral composed primarily of sodium chloride and is one of the universal tastes in fast food. It is an important food preservative. Salt regulates the fluids in our body and every living creature needs sodium and chloride, plants and animals alike, but only in small amounts.

It's a crystalline solid, white or sometimes pale pink or light grey, and is processed from sea water or rock deposits. The greyish colour in edible rock salt comes from the mineral content of the rock and this is different to mineral salt that comes from plant sources (celery is the most common, it makes a superb salt alternative and the minerals in celery help balance the body).

Salt is such a valuable commodity it has been used as a currency in trade. Roman soldiers were paid in salt, in Greece slaves were traded for salt, in Ethiopia salt bars were standard currently until quite recently, hence the sayings, "not worth one's salt" or "the salt of the earth".

We only need a very small amount of salt in our diets, preferably sea salt, and too much salt in your diet may cause dark circles under your eyes.

Salt used for human consumption comes in three forms: unrefined salt (sea salt), refined salt (table salt) and iodized salt. Sea salt is the most beneficial because it has the ability to restore balance to our body's fluids, unlike table salt, which is refined by adding aluminosilicate or sodium, or yellow prussiate of soda plus bleaches to make sure the salt is free flowing, but the problem here is that this free flowing salt is unable to combine with human body fluids.

Salt also makes us thirsty, which is why it's used as an ingredient in soft drinks – the answer to why soft drinks don't necessarily quench your thirst.

Salt has many uses and some surprising applications. It can be dyed and used to create artwork. It's a great way to keep an artificial floral arrangement in place – just fill your vase with salt, add a little bit of cold water and put your floral arrangement together.

The salt will set hard as it dries keeping the flowers in place.

The old wives' tale of making water boil faster by putting a pinch of salt into the pot doesn't hold water (pardon the pun), however a pinch of salt in water does make water boil at a higher temperature, which is why salted water works so well with poaching eggs; it raises the temperature and sets the whites faster.

# Washing Soda

Not to be confused with washing powder, which is a powdered soap and detergent; washing soda, closely related to baking soda, is a highly alkaline chemical compound that is fantastic as a cleaning agent.

Washing soda is also known as sodium carbonate and is also called soda ash; this is because one of the main sources of washing soda comes from the ash of plants.

As the name infers, washing soda's most common use is in the laundry as the high alkalinity helps it act as a solvent to remove stains.

But its ability goes well beyond the laundry. It doesn't stain like bleach, is a brilliant de-scaler and anything that's hard to clean due to mineral build up will clean in no time with washing soda.

Textile artists use washing soda to help dyes adhere to fabric, which in turn gives the fabric longer lasting colour (colourfast).

Washing soda is a heavy hitting cleaner that is perfect for stoves and any job that has most other cleaning products beat.

Just a note of warning though; washing soda is caustic in large doses, so label it well and keep it out of reach of little hands and pets. Be careful not to inhale it and make sure you wear gloves when handling.

# Lemon Alternatives

Many plants taste or smell similar to lemons and can serve as either flavour or scent substitutes, though they cannot necessarily mimic lemon's cleansing and antiseptic properties.

+ Certain cultivars of basil such as lemon basil (also known as Indonesian basil), Thai lemon basil, and lime basil, are used in Asian cooking.

+ Certain cultivars of mint such as lemon balm and lemon mint (also known as purple horsemint), when crushed emit a lemony scent.

+ Lemongrass (Cymbopogon) is a genus of 55 species of grasses native to warm and tropical climates. Lemongrass is commonly used in teas, soups and curries in Asian cuisine. Its oil is sometimes used as a pesticide and preservative as well as a lure for honeybees.

+ Lemon myrtle (or lemon scented ironwood or sweet verbena tree) is native to the subtropical rainforests of Queensland, Australia. It is cultivated for cooking and as an essential oil. The dried leaf has antioxidant properties.

+ Lemon thyme smells and tastes like lemon. Its tiny leaves can be used in any recipes that call for lemons, even marinades.

+ Lemon verbena is a shrub whose leaves emit a lemon scent when bruised and is considered the most strongly scented of the lemon scented plants. It is used as a lemon substitute in cooking and in place of actual lemon in tea infusions. It has strong antioxidant properties.

+ A note about Limes – Lemons and limes, both citrus fruits, share some similar properties but are not the same. Limes are green in colour and smaller than lemons. They also have a bittersweet taste to lemon's sour. Limes do not have the same high concentration of vitamin C, so they are a weak substitute for lemon's astringent properties, but their scent can be a pleasant addition to cleaning products.

# Vinegar in History

+ As early as 5000 BC, the Babylonians produced vinegar by fermenting the fruit of date palms.

+ The ancient Greek doctor, Hippocrates, father of modern medicine, prescribed vinegar to his patients.

+ The ancient Romans made vinegar from grapes, figs, dates, and rye. The word vinegar comes from the Latin words *vinum*, meaning wine, and *acer*, meaning sour.

+ In 41 BC, Cleopatra, the last pharaoh of ancient Egypt, wagered with Mark Antony, one of the rulers of Rome, that she could host the most lavish meal in history. To accomplish this, at the conclusion of the day-long meal, Cleopatra removed one of her pearl earrings and dropped it in a goblet of wine vinegar. The pearl dissolved, and Cleopatra drank the vinegar with the extraordinarily valuable pearl, and Antony conceded defeat.

+ Evidence of Sherry vinegar dates as far back as the first century AD. It is produced in the Spanish province of Cadiz. The production and quality of true Sherry vinegar are strictly controlled by Spain and the European Union.

+ Around 1,000 years ago, the Chinese developed a rice water vinegar called Chencu, or mature vinegar. It is used as flavouring in Chinese cuisine.

+ Vinegar making has been a registered trade in France since the reign of Charles VI, who ruled as "The Mad King" from 1380-1422.

+ During the Middle Ages, vinegar was used medicinally for washing and treating illnesses such as the plague, leprosy, and snake bites.

+ Balsamic vinegar is traditionally produced in the Italian town of Modena, where its existence was documented as early as 1046. True balsamic vinegars have protected designations under both Italian and European Union production codes. The inferior "balsamic vinegar of Modena" is a modern imitation that is widely available and much less expensive than aged balsamics.

+ Victorian prostitutes used vinegar as a cheap (yet unreliable) contraceptive.

# THE VERSATILITY OF TEA TREE OIL

**TEA TREE OIL** is obtained by steam distilling the leaves of the tea tree (*Melaleuca alternifolia*) – not to be confused with the unrelated common tea plant (*Camellia sinensis*) that is used to make black and green tea. The tea tree is native to Queensland and New South Wales, Australia. It was named by eighteenth century sailors who made tea that smelled like nutmeg from the leaves of the tree growing on the marshes and swamps of the southeast Australian coast.

Thought of as a natural cure-all, the chemicals in tea tree oil may kill bacteria and fungus and reduce allergic skin reactions. Tea tree oil contains *terpenoids*, which are chemically modified *terpenes* – organic compounds found to have antiseptic and antifungal activity. The compound *terpinen-4-ol* is the most abundant terpene in tea tree leaves and is thought to be responsible for most of the essential oil's antimicrobial activity. Tea tree oil is a common ingredient in deodorants, shampoos, soaps and lotions.

Tea tree oil is applied to the skin (used topically) for infections such as acne, fungal infections of the nail

> The chemicals in tea tree oil may kill bacteria and fungus and reduce allergic skin reactions

(*onychomycosis*), lice, scabies, athlete's foot (*tinea pedis*), and ringworm. It is also used topically as a local antiseptic for cuts and abrasions, burns, insect bites and stings, boils, toothache, infections of the mouth and nose, and sore throat, among other ailments. Some people add it to bath water to treat cough, bronchial congestion and pulmonary inflammation, although eucalyptus oil (see below) might be a more powerful respiratory remedy.

Tea tree oil is safe for most people when applied to the skin, but it can cause skin irritation and swelling in some cases, especially in large doses. For people treating acne, it can sometimes cause skin dryness, itching, stinging, burning and redness. Occasionally, people may have allergic reactions to tea tree oil, ranging from mild contact dermatitis to severe blisters and rashes. Undiluted tea tree oil may cause skin irritation, redness, blistering and itching.

### Special precautions & warnings:

Please be advised that although its low toxicity and wide range of applications make it an ideal natural remedy, tea tree oil can have side effects. Studies show that contact with tea tree oil may alter hormone levels, causing unexplained breast enlargement in boys who have not yet reached puberty. People with hormone-sensitive cancers or pregnant or nursing women should avoid tea tree oil. It is unsafe when taken by mouth (orally). As a general rule, never take tea tree oil or any undiluted essential oils by mouth due to the possibility of serious side effects. Taking tree tea oil orally has caused confusion, inability to walk, unsteadiness, rash, and coma.

# Basic Tea Tree Oil Solution

Use this solution as a room deodoriser, mildew repellent (though it will not remove previous discoloration from grout), a disinfectant spray or as a mould remover (do not wipe away).

▶ Mix 15 drops of tea tree oil per 500ml of water, pour into a spray bottle and shake well.

# Undiluted Tea Tree Oil

A few drops of tea tree oil in your dishwasher dispenser will help remove the residue that builds up on your dishes.

▶ Adding a few drops to your humidifier will not only emit a clean, refreshing scent into the air, but it will also disinfect a sickroom.

▶ Add a few drops to your laundry as a freshener and disinfectant.

▶ Tea tree oil is an excellent insect repellent. Wipe down your kitchen work surfaces and cabinets with a simple solution of soapy water and a few drops of tea tree oil to keep the bugs at bay. Do the same for any hard floors, paying attention the corners and trims. Your room will smell just-cleaned and the pests will stay away.

# Cosmetic Uses

Simple Healing Ointment – Mix 5ml of a non-allergenic cream base, such as calendula cream, with two to three drops of tea tree oil and rub on affected areas such as cuts, blisters or rough patches of skin.

▶ Scalp Rub/Dandruff Treatment – To condition your hair and scalp as well as to combat dandruff and itchy scalp, rub 10 drops of tea tree oil with your fingertips into the scalp between shampoos.

▶ Barber's Rash – Also called shaving rash, it's characterised by a mass of small red pimples on the face and neck, and is exacerbated by shaving, of course. To counteract the irritation caused by your razor, rinse the affected areas with warm water containing a few drops of tea tree oil. For a more direct approach, add 10 to 12 drops of tea tree oil to a 50ml bottle of lavender water* and shake well. Dab the affected areas with the solution using cotton balls.

*Please refer to the Aromatherapy section of this book for a simple lavender water recipe.*

# EUCALYPTUS: A MIRACLE EVERGREEN

**EUCALYPTUS IS A** genus of flowering trees and shrubs in the myrtle family. Nearly all eucalyptus trees are evergreen (having leaves all seasons), but some tropical species lose their leaves after the dry season ends. Most species of eucalyptus are native to Australia, though they are cultivated throughout the world in temperate climates where it does not frost. They are fast-growing producers of wood, and their copious consumption of water makes them a natural insecticide because they drain swamps that attract mosquitoes, which spread malaria. The Australian Blue Mountains take their name from the haze created by the mist emitted by the trees' vaporising leaves, which contain ample amounts of volatile (rapidly evaporating) oil.

Eucalyptus trees are a source of pulpwood, which is converted into the pulp used to make paper. Their trunks, when hollowed out by termites, are used to make the didgeridoo, a traditional Aboriginal wind instrument, and the nectar of certain species is used to produce high quality honey. All parts of the eucalyptus can be used to produce dyes in colours ranging from yellow, orange and red to green, tan and rust.

Eucalyptus oil is distilled from the tree's leaves and has many medicinal and household uses such as relieving congestion and disinfecting clothing and surfaces. In addition to the applications for eucalyptus oil found throughout the book, its industrial applications include serving as a fragrance component in soaps, detergents and perfumes, as well as an ingredient in ethanol and petrol fuels.

Its health and beauty properties are discussed in the Aromatherapy section of this book, but here is an easy recipe for a natural, eucalyptus-based insect repellent.

Spray it on yourself and around the outdoor area where you plan to camp or picnic. The scent of eucalyptus should keep the mosquitoes and ticks away, and it is safe to use around children and pets. Just remember to keep it away from your eyes.

## Eucalyptus Insect Repellent Spray

500ml of water
2 capfuls (or 10ml) of liquid soap
10-25 drops of eucalyptus oil
Dark spray bottle

Mix the ingredients and pour them into the spray bottle, making sure to shake the contents before each use. Reapply every hour and after swimming or exercise.

The scent of eucalyptus should keep the mosquitoes and ticks away

# GRAPEFRUIT: LEMON'S POWERFUL COUSIN

**THE EXISTENCE OF** the grapefruit tree was first documented in Barbados, where it was known as the "forbidden fruit". Like its citrus cousin the lemon, it is a wonder fruit, as all parts of the grapefruit have uses. The pulp is consumed whole and also squeezed for its tangy juice. It is a good source of vitamin C, and the pink and red varieties contain the antioxidant lycopene, which helps to remove free radicals – thought to cause many cancers – from your body. Lycopene is also believed to play a role in the prevention of heart disease by preventing LDL cholesterol from being oxidised.

And most anyone who's attempted to eliminate that "spare tire" knows that grapefruit's low glycemic index helps the body's metabolism burn fat.

Grapefruit seed extract (GSE), also known as citrus seed extract, is believed to have strong antimicrobial properties against fungi and bacteria. It is a liquid derived from the seeds, pulp, and white membranes of the grapefruit. Homemade GSE can be produced by grinding the seed and juiceless pulp of the grapefruit and mixing them with glycerine, but the process can be fairly difficult. Commercially manufactured GSE will suit your needs just fine.

# GSE Natural Cleaner and Sanitiser

Use this mixture as a natural means of preventing the spread of E. coli, Salmonella, Staphylococcus, Streptococcus and other bacteria and germs. It also cleans and brightens hard surfaces.

Mix 15 drops of GSE per 500ml of water. (Double the amount of GSE per 500ml of water for heavy-duty jobs.) Pour into a spray bottle and use the solution to disinfect things such as plastic children's toys, playpens, door knobs, and garbage bins. Spray the solution onto your sinks, tubs and tiles, allowing it to sit for at least 15 seconds. Wiping the solution away should reveal whiter and brighter surfaces.

# GRAPEFRUIT JUICE
# HOUSEHOLD CLEANSER

If you read the ingredient list on expensive commercial cleaners, you'll notice that many manufacturers use grapefruit in their products. Using fresh juice in a home-made alternative will give you pure cleaning power. You will still get the anti-viral and anti-microbial properties of the commercial cleansers, while making a product that is safe for children and pets and avoiding the unwanted respiratory reactions commercial cleaners can induce. Use this mixture to clean work surfaces, tubs, sinks and hard floors. It is also ideal for items baby comes into contact with like toys and cribs, and any other sensitive areas.

Combine one part freshly squeezed grapefruit juice with one part vinegar and three parts hot water. Wipe down or mop surfaces and let air dry.

# let's have some fun

## EVERYTHING WE DO, TO SOME DEGREE, RELIES ON **ACTION** AND **REACTION**.

**CHEMICAL REACTION** is what makes the world go around – ask anyone looking for romance and they'll tell you the importance of chemistry in a relationship.

Playing around with chemistry is a good way to see how and why things work – it's a visual example of how the ingredients in cleaning products work their magic in our drains and on our benches.

So let's have some fun with how things mix and match.

# ELEPHANT TOOTHPASTE

This one has no purpose whatsoever other than entertainment value. Although it does show the awesome marriage of simple household ingredients creating a frothy foam that looks just like toothpaste.

It's harmless so can be washed down the drain without any problems and it will clean the drain on the way down.

**YOU'LL NEED:**

125ml of Hydrogen Peroxide (6%) (You can buy this at the supermarket or chemist)
1 sachet of dry powdered yeast + 4 tbsp of warm water
Food colouring if you want it to look pretty
Some detergent
An empty plastic bottle (a soft drink bottle is perfect)
A tray to catch the overflow (baking dish is perfect)
A funnel for pouring the ingredients into the bottle
A pair of safety goggles

1. Put the dry yeast into a cup and add the 4 tbsp of warm water. Stir until mixed.

2. Using the funnel pour 125ml of 6% hydrogen peroxide into the empty bottle (add your food colouring at this stage).

3. Swirl the bottle to mix the food colouring evenly (if you used any).

4. Pour yeast solution into the plastic bottle with hydrogen peroxide and watch it start to produce foam.

This should produce approximately 2 litres of foam. The foam will be warm because the experiment produces a certain amount of heat, but it's completely safe to touch.

As the foam expands it will ooze out of the top of the bottle not unlike toothpaste oozing out of the end of the tube.

Great fun, the kids will love it.

# FUN LAVA LAMP

This shows how carbon dioxide gas is formed, and is the principle behind quite a few cleaning products.

In this one you see the bubbles rise to the surface taking kernels of corn with them. You can watch the corn go up and down for ages. It's very relaxing, almost better than watching fish in a tank.

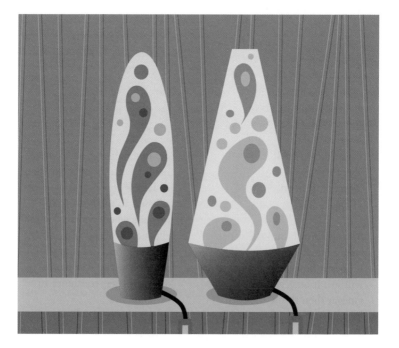

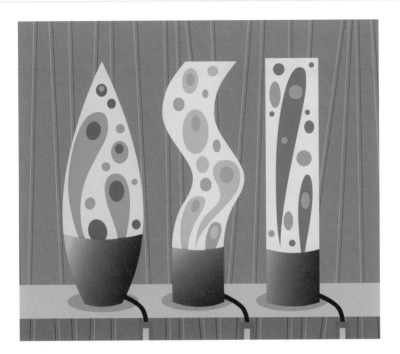

**YOU'LL NEED:**

A big spoon of
bicarbonate of soda
A glass of water
Some vinegar
A handful of dried
corn kernels
(popping corn
is perfect)

1. Mix the bicarb into the water with a quick stir (don't worry if it doesn't dissolve, the vinegar will sort it out), add some vinegar then throw the corn kernels in.

2. The carbon dioxide bubbles formed by mixing bicarb and vinegar will stick to the corn kernels, the bubbles rise to the top dragging the corn with them. When they hit the air the bubbles break and the corn will sink to the bottom of the glass where another bubble will stick to it and take it back up to the top. And so it goes, up – down – up – down, as long as the gas continues to form bubbles.

# THE UNSINKABLE BUBBLES

The kids will love this one; these bubbles won't sink even if you bounce them.

**YOU'LL NEED:**

A clear jar or big vase, anything with a wide opening at the top
Some bicarb soda
Some vinegar

Some bubble mix and a bubble ring (the ring off the top of a milk bottle will do if you don't have a proper bubble ring, but every house needs a bubble ring, they are so much fun)

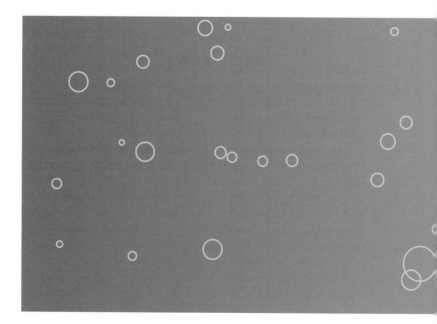

1. Put a few spoons of bicarb soda into the jar and pour in enough vinegar so the bubbles created reach half way up the jar.

2. When the bubbles settle down a bit give the mixture a good swish around to help the bicarb dissolve.

3. Take the bubble ring and bubble mix and blow some bubbles. Blow them nice and high and when they fall catch some in the jar – the bubbles won't sink to the bottom no matter what you do.

As we found out from the lava lamp, bicarb soda and vinegar mixed together make carbon dioxide gas, and because carbon dioxide is heavier than air it sinks to the bottom of the jar. The bubble is full of air so it floats on the heavier carbon dioxide and no matter what you do you won't be able to get it to sink to the bottom of the jar.

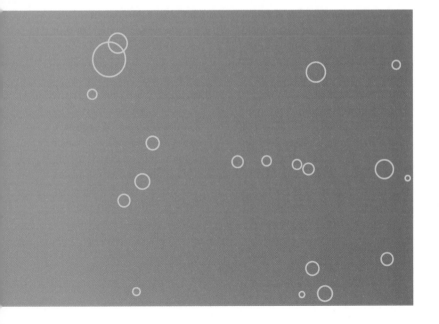

# MINI ROCKET

Here's a great one for the kids but make sure you watch them carefully, children can get a bit excited when they have the chance to blow something up – everyone likes a bit of an explosion.

## YOU'LL NEED:

**1 tbsp of vinegar**
**½ tbsp of bicarb soda**
**A plastic film canister**
  **with a lid**

1. Go outside where you have plenty of space.

2. Put the vinegar into the film canister then add the bicarb soda.

3. Jam the lid on quickly.

4. Turn the canister upside down and run for cover.

**WARNING:** *Run for cover, the canister will launch skyward pretty quickly and although it doesn't launch with the power of a missile you don't want to be in the line of fire. Make sure no-one stands over the canister or points it at anyone.*

As previously mentioned, when bicarb and vinegar are mixed together they make carbon dioxide gas. Gases can be compressed into really small spaces and build pressure so when carbon dioxide gas is produced inside the closed canister the gas can't escape and pressure builds up enough to blow the lid off.

This is the principle behind carbonated drinks (soft drinks), which are made when carbon dioxide is dissolved under pressure in water. While the lid is on the bottle pressure is maintained but when the bottle is opened pressure is reduced and the bubbles of carbon dioxide, which are lighter than water, rise to the surface; the fizz sound when the bottle is opened.

# kitchen

## START YOUR **GREEN CLEANING REVOLUTION** IN THE HEART OF THE HOME

**THEY SAY THE KITCHEN** is the heart of the home, so why not start your green cleaning revolution here? The kitchen is also one of the most important rooms in the house to keep clean as it's where you prepare your and your family's meals, making safe cleaning a high priority. Don't risk your family's health with the chemical cocktails that can be found in mainstream cleaners, follow these simple recipes to keep benches, ovens, drains, dishwashers and yes even the kitchen sink sparkling.

# SIMPLE HOMEMADE LIQUID DETERGENT

1. Decant 500ml of liquid soap (see page 12).

2. Store in a squeeze top bottle and use as needed. A few big squirts will do a large wash and if you want loads of suds squirt the liquid directly under the tap and turn the tap on full. The stronger the water pressure, the more bubbles you'll get.

If you are in an area where the water is hard, add 2 tbsp of washing soda dissolved in ⅓ cup of water to the soap mixture, and if you have greasy washing up to do add 2 tbsp of bicarb to the liquid soap or the juice of half a lemon.

Now the thing about homemade washing up detergent is that it may not be 100% streak free. It won't be far off but there could be some residue on glassware; plates will be fine, but glassware may not gleam like diamonds without a bit of help. The chemical companies have it down pat; you literally don't need to dry your dishes because they do it for you in their formulation.

A few big squirts will do a large wash and if you want loads of suds squirt the liquid directly under the tap and turn the tap on full

Any residue left on glassware can be wiped off quickly while the dishes are put away and here's where the old fashioned tea-towel comes into play. Manual wiping up is good bonding time for siblings, time for chatting about the day, sharing some juicy gossip from school, and with the prospect of a bit of tea towel flicking there's never an argument about who's on drying-up duty.

# BASIC ALL PURPOSE KITCHEN AND BENCH CLEANER

½ tsp of baking soda
½ tsp of borax
2 tbsp of vinegar
½ tsp of liquid soap
   (see page 12)
2 cups of water

1. Combine all ingredients in a spray bottle (feel free to use your previous all purpose cleaner bottle, just make sure it has been rinsed very well) and shake until all the ingredients are combined.

2. Spray then wipe clean with a damp cloth.

TIPS:
*You can add a few drops of essential oil to give your cleaner a lovely scent. A tiny sprinkle of lemon rind is also a lovely natural scent to use.*

If you find that you require stronger cleaning power, just increase the amount of borax by 1 tsp.

## FOR A
# QUICK FIX

Sprinkle bicarb soda onto the surface you want to clean. Spray with a solution of water and vinegar at a ratio of 1:3. Wipe dry.

# Kitchen cupboards

Use vinegar or lemon juice diluted in warm water to wipe spills and marks on cupboard shelves. The vinegar will kill any bacteria that may be lurking ready to multiply and it will also help prevent mould and mildew.

Usually ¼ cup of either vinegar or lemon juice together with 1 cup of warm water is a good ratio.

# For stubborn stains

For stubborn stains put a few drops of lemon juice on the stain and leave it to sit for a few minutes before sprinkling bicarb over and scrubbing gently. Rinse with water.

## TO REMOVE
# MAGIC MARKER FROM SURFACES

Hopefully you won't encounter the accidental magic marker on bench surfaces very often, as they can be hard to remove, but try spraying the mark with hair spray then wipe it clean.

# DRAIN CLEANER

This is a great one for the kids, they'll love cleaning the drains for you once they've discovered the fun to be had with the mysterious fizzing, bubbling monster lurking down the drain.

¼ **cup of bicarb soda**
½ **cup of white vinegar**

Make sure the sink is dry otherwise the bicarb clumps and is hard to get down the plug hole. If it clumps just break it up and push it through, it just takes a bit longer.

1. Pour the bicarb soda into the drain.

2. Pour the vinegar down the drain hole (a bit at a time).

3. Put the plug in and let everything sit for 15 -30 minutes to work its magic then pour hot water down the drain to make sure everything is washed through.

4. If your drain is particularly sluggish you can repeat the process, the best way to know when to stop adding vinegar is when the fizzing stops.

# To get rid of fingerprints on stainless steel fridges and ovens

It doesn't matter how many times you tell the kids to keep their gorgeous sticky little fingers off the shiny stainless steel fridge doors, you'll always find some little tell-tale signs of in-between snacking.

▶ To keep the fridge door free of fingerprints wipe with a soft cloth that has been dabbed with a small amount of baby oil. Keep the cloth somewhere handy and you never know; you may even be able to tempt the phantom-fingerprint bandit to do the job for you.

# To clean your microwave

**2 tbsp of lemon juice
  or vinegar
4 cups of water**

1. Mix water and lemon juice together in a large microwave safe bowl.

2. Microwave on high for 3 - 4 minutes.

3. Allow the steam to condense on the inside walls.

4. Remove the bowl (careful, it will be hot) and wipe the inside of the microwave with a clean cloth.

5. Repeat to get rid of stubborn spots.

# Powder for your dishwasher

Make up a powder for the dishwasher by mixing equal parts of bicarb with borax and use 2 tbsp per load.

— OR —

▶ Mix 1 cup borax with 1 cup bicarb soda, ¼ cup of salt and ¼ cup of citric acid. You can also add a few drops of essential oils but this is optional.

▶ Store in an airtight plastic container and use 1 tbsp per load.

# Dishwasher odours and soap build-up

Splash 1 cup of vinegar around the inside of the empty machine then run a cycle without any dishes. If you do this once a month it will keep your machine smelling fresh and free from soap scum.

▶ It works just as well if you run it through a full load and saves wasting water.

## TO REMOVE
# KITCHEN ODOURS

No-one likes unpleasant smells wafting through the kitchen, here are a few tips for cheap and effective air fresheners.

## Refrigerator and cupboards

Keep an open box of bicarb soda in your fridge, cupboards or anywhere you would like to remove offending odours. Bicarb has the most amazing ability to absorb odours and will stay effective for ages. You can re-use the bicarb to make a cleaning paste or oven cleaner after it's done its job as an odour eater.

## Bench top compost and wheelie bins

You can also sprinkle bicarb in your garbage cans and bench top compost bins to keep them smelling fresh.

# Food containers and lunch boxes

There are a few quick ways to get rid of the stale smell that builds up in re-used food containers and lunch boxes.

▶ Soak a piece of sliced bread in vinegar and put it into the container, put the lid on and leave overnight. In the morning remove the bread and rinse the container under the tap.

▶ Sprinkle bicarb soda around inside of the container and rinse in hot water. If the smell is particularly strong, rather than rinsing the container leave a mixture of water and bicarb in the container overnight and rinse in the morning.

▶ Wipe the container over with a cloth drench in white vinegar then rinse.

▶ If your container is microwave safe put some water into the container with half a lemon and microwave for 2 minutes on high, leave to cool before removing then wash in warm soapy water.

# Remove odours from jars

If you keep glass jars for re-use but find some retain the smell of past ingredients simply pour some strong black coffee into the jar, put the lid on loosely, leave for a while, empty and rinse with water. Any odour will go out with the coffee. It's also a great way to use leftover coffee.

# Remove odour from your garbage disposal unit

Pour ½ cup of sea salt down your disposal followed by a few ice cubes then run the cold water and start the disposal. The ice will help dislodge all the chunky bits and the salt will remove odours.

# General odour-eater

To mask general odours burn some coffee beans in a saucepan, but not enough to damage the saucepan. The strong coffee smell overpowers any other smell lurking around.

## TO GET RID OF THE LINGERING SMELL OF FISH

A thick fillet of fried fish makes a great meal but what isn't so great is the lingering fishy smell that permeates the kitchen and adjoining rooms; not quite up there with cooked cabbage but it gets pretty close.

Here's a handy tip to get rid of the fishy smell so you can enjoy your meal without having to breathe in the aftermath.

As soon as you take the fish out of the pan throw in a blob of peanut butter. Don't ask me how it works but it absorbs the lingering odour instantly.

# OVENS AND STOVES

## Hate cleaning the oven? Most of us do.

Here are a few recipes for oven cleaners that work a treat, have a play around to find the one you prefer and when your oven is sparkling like new keep it that way by wiping it over with a cloth doused in vinegar after each use (preferably before it cools down completely). The vinegar stops fat sticking so your job becomes easier and easier – almost like a self cleaning oven.

These recipes work as well, if not better, than the chemical oven cleaners on the market and best of all they're free of Butane, Monoethanolamine, Diethylene Glycol Monobutyl Ether, Sodium Hydroxide and Diethanolamine, which commercial products may contain. No-one needs to take the risk of breathing any of those into their lungs.

## Oven door

To clean a grease splattered oven door, use a cloth saturated with white vinegar, full strength this time, wipe the problem area and leave the oven door open for 15-20 minutes before rinsing with a damp sponge.

# Strong oven cleaner

**1 cup of ammonia**
**1 cup of water**
**1 oven proof bowl (keep**
**an eye out at charity shops**
**for some old bowls to use**
**for cleaning jobs)**

1. Mix water and ammonia in an oven proof bowl.

2. Place bowl in warmed oven for 15 minutes.

3. Remove the bowl from the oven and discard water/ammonia mixture.

4. Sprinkle some bicarb on a wet cloth and wipe away excess grease and grime.

Ammonia releases fumes when warmed so make sure you open a window (or two) and it's a good idea to cover your nose and mouth so you don't breath the fumes in as they are toxic.

If you'd prefer something without a strong smell the following recipe works just as well.

# To keep your oven sparkling clean and grease free

Wipe the oven with a damp cloth soaked in diluted white vinegar. If you do this regularly the grease and fat from cooking won't stick to the oven walls and it will make it easier to keep clean.

It only takes a second to give the oven a wipe over and if you have just cleaned the oven with a strong smelling cleaning agent the vinegar will get rid of the smell so it won't taint your next meal.

If there is some build-up on the oven walls or floor shake some bicarb soda onto a soft scourer and give it a quick wipe, then rinse clean and finish off with a vinegar treatment.

Have a play around to find the oven cleaner you prefer

# To clean the bottom of your oven

This is always a problem area; especially if spilled food is left to re-bake (it's so much easier to wipe the oven clean after each use).

This is an easy remedy but before you start make sure the oven is cold and cover any elements with foil or something to protect them.

1. Using an atomizer full of water, spray the bottom of the oven.
2. Sprinkle bicarb soda over the oven floor.
3. Give it a few more squirts of water from the atomizer.
4. Leave overnight and wipe over with a damp cloth.
5. Rinse with hot water.

If the oven floor has a lot of caked on residue you may need to repeat this a few times.

Once the oven floor is clean give it a final rinse over with vinegar to stop grease sticking.

# To clean a spill on the bottom of the oven

We've all done it – had a casserole or pie bubble over spilling food all over the bottom of the oven. Best to attack it before it bakes and sets hard.

Cover the spill with a handful of salt. Salt doesn't smoke or smell under heat and it will bake into a crust that makes it easier to clean the mess up (but wait until it cools down, no point in getting burned fingers).

## TO CLEAN
# YOUR SINK

Nothing beats bicarb soda to give a mirror shine to your sink. Make a paste of bicarb soda and water and apply with a cloth then wipe over and rinse, or sprinkle bicarb soda directly onto a damp cloth, wipe over and then rinse off. Either method works well; it's just a matter of what suits you.

## Kitchen windows, backsplashes and floors

Kitchen windows, backsplashes and floors all have one thing in common – they are the target for grease and fat splatters from cooking.

Vinegar stops grease and fat sticking and makes cleaning easier so use vinegar when you are cleaning glass or the backsplash and throw some in the final rinse when you're doing the floor and you'll find cleaning much easier next time around.

## Scouring powder

This is abrasive for those stubborn areas and is not suitable for laminated bench tops, glass top hot plates or any surface that might scratch.

Mix equal parts of bicarb soda, borax and salt together to use as a scouring powder to remove heavy grease and dirt.

## TO REMOVE
# GREASE FROM POTS AND PANS

Save yourself that awful job of getting grease out of pans and reduce water wastage at the same time. Simply sprinkle the pot, pan or BBQ plate with salt and leave the salt to do its work of absorbing. Wipe with paper towel and you'll find all the grease will have been absorbed and you can wash your pan with the rest of the dishes without contaminating the rest of the washing up with an unpleasant greasy film.

# To remove burnt food from cooking pans

One old fashioned cleaning method was to put burnt saucepans and dishes upside down on top of an ant hill and leave them for the industrious little fellows to slowly munch their way through the burnt food until the pans and dishes were clean. Worked well, but it took a while, here's an easier and faster method.

**¼ cup of bicarb soda**
**2 tbsp salt**
**Hot water (enough to make a thick paste)**

1. Make a paste of the bicarb, salt and water.

2. Use a damp cloth and wipe the paste over the pan or if you are cleaning the oven (keep away from wires and heating elements).

3. Let the paste sit for at least 5 – 10 minutes (can leave for up to 20 minutes but make sure that the paste is not too dry to start with).

4. Rinse with warm water and a cloth.

For tough stains, scrub with fine steel wool and some more baking soda. It's always best not to use steel wool unless absolutely necessary, loosening grease and grime is always better for the surfaces than scrubbing, once they have been scrubbed they become harder to clean.

— OR —

▶ Try rhubarb; juice the stalks and use the juice to wipe over the burn, or boil some chopped rhubarb in a very small amount of water, simmer gently, leave overnight then wipe clean.

## AND SPEAKING OF BURNING

Salt always held a place of honour in Grandma's kitchen. The salt jar wasn't so much an indication of how much salt Granny used in cooking because salt has many uses as a scourer, mouth gargle, as well as an aid to cooking, and it was no accident that the salt pot was kept near the stove.

Salt is a brilliant fire extinguisher for grease fires, it acts like a heat blanket, dissipating the heat and starving the fire of oxygen. In an emergency a handful of dirt will do the same but by the time you've come back in from the yard the fire could well have taken hold.

So if you like homemade deep fried chips follow Granny's lead and keep a big accessible jar of salt near the stove just in case.

# Kitchen disinfectant

**YOU'LL NEED:**

1 cup of water
1 cup of white vinegar
20-30 drops of tea tree oil
    or eucalyptus oil

Mix all ingredients together in a spray bottle and use when needed.

# To clean and disinfect wooden cutting boards

Use a spray bottle to spay your boards with full strength white vinegar. Vinegar is a fantastic disinfectant and will protect your wooden boards from the harmful bugs E. coli, salmonella and staphylococcus, and it works on plastic cutting boards just as effectively.

# To remove garlic and onion smells from your wooden boards

Rub half a lemon over the board and wipe down with some paper towel.

— OR —

▶ Rub your board with coarse salt or bicarb soda. Leave it for a few minutes then rinse.

— OR —

▶ If you live somewhere sunny, once you have washed your board, put it out in the sun for a few hours (make sure you turn it so both sides get a good hit of sunshine). Let the sunshine work its magic.

*If you live somewhere sunny, put it out in the sun for a few hours (make sure you turn it)*

# A few helpful notes on the care of wooden cutting boards

Bacteria lives in the moisture that is on your boards, so make sure your boards are nice and dry when you're not using them. I lean mine up against the back of our drying rack so that only a small part of the board is touching the bench. This ensures that the whole board dries at the same time.

▶ I only ever use my wood board for chopping vegetables, bread etc, but never meat. If I want to chop meat on it I either cover my board with parchment paper so I can throw it away later or use some cheap plastic mats. I still use my wooden board underneath because I like the solid feel but the plastic mats can go in the dishwasher afterwards and my wooden board is safe from cross contamination.

▶ Never leave your wooden boards submerged in hot water. Wood is porous and will soak up water, which is bad for cracking and also creates a breeding ground for bacteria.

## TO REMOVE **GARLIC** AND **ONION SMELLS** FROM YOUR HANDS

If your skin has picked up garlic or onion smells rub your hands on stainless steel before you wash them, the sink is ideal and you'll be surprised at how effective this trick is.

Alternatively you can use lemon or bicarb. They will work just as well on your hands as they do on wooden cutting boards.

## To disinfect your wooden spoons

Soak them in a ratio of 1 part bleach to 20 parts water for 15 minutes. Rinse and resoak in warm soapy water for 15 minutes to remove the bleach smell. Wash as normal and dry completely.

Your wooden spoons are similar to your cutting boards and will absorb some of the liquids they stir. It's a good idea to give them a good disinfecting every now and then, this will kill the bugs but also extend the lifespan of your utensils.

Avoid putting your wooden utensils in the dishwasher, it will shorten their lifespan and help absorb other contaminants that may be in your washing load.

# To extend the life of your kitchen sponges

There is a lot of hype about the hygiene of using kitchen sponges. One ad would have us believe using a kitchen sponge is like wiping your benches with a piece of raw chicken. But there is nothing wrong with using sponges providing you are diligent with keeping them in good condition.

▶ Here's a quick way to extend their life, save on paper towel use and also make sure that your sponges are hygienic.

▶ Make up a solution of ⅓ cup of salt and ½ cup of vinegar per 1 litre of water. Soak your sponges overnight in this solution and they'll be restored to their former glory and be free from bacteria.

▶ Germs love to live in warm, moist environments so when you're not using your sponges make sure you put them on the draining rack to dry thoroughly, also leave them in the sun as often as you can.

▶ Here's another quick method for those with a microwave. Wet the sponge, squeeze the excess water out and put it in the microwave on high for 2 minutes. The heat will kill any bacteria but remember the sponges will be hot and will hold the heat for a while so wait until they have cooled before you attempt to take them out.

# EASY METHOD TO CLEAN UP **BROKEN EGGS**

We've all tried to scoop up an egg that has dropped on the floor and struggled with getting the floor completely clean and disposing of the mess on the sponge. Here's a much easier way.

Cover the broken egg with salt and let the salt draw the egg together. Then just wipe it up with some paper towel.

# Easy method for picking up broken glass

If you have broken glass and are worried that you haven't picked up all of the splinters, use a thick piece of soft bread and wipe over the area where you think the glass may be. The bread will catch even the smallest splinters.

▶ Please be sure you seal the glass laden bread before you discard it into the rubbish bin to avoid any hungry scavengers at the tip eating it.

# To remove stains from coffee and tea cups or a coffee pot

**YOU'LL NEED:**

**¼ cup of salt**
**3 tbsp of lemon juice
   or white vinegar**
**Some ice cubes**

Mix all ingredients together in a pouring jug, pour some into each cup, swish the mixture around and rinse. The ice cubes combined with the salt and lemon/vinegar work together to remove any stains.

# laundry

## CHEAP AND EFFECTIVE HOMEMADE LAUNDRY DETERGENTS

**IF WE BELIEVED** everything we see on TV we would think that only commercial detergents can give a good clean wash. But this is far from the truth. Those special 'lifters' and 'new' or 'improved' formulas are merely marketing gimmicks.

The pioneers strained wood ash through straw to collect lye, which was then mixed with animal fat for heavy duty soap; effective but very drying on the hands.

We've come a long way since then but traditionally laundry soap was always made at home until early last century when it was marketed as a convenient commercial product and the old homemade recipes lost favour.

However, these commercial products were merely a duplicate of homemade products and have never really been improved.

# Laundry detergent suitable for machines and hand washing

Mix 1 litre of liquid soap (see page 12) with 2 tbsp of washing soda dissolved in 1 cup of water and 1 tbsp of bicarb soda.

▶ Use 1 cup per medium load. Use more for heavily soiled clothes.

▶ If you have hard water add a bit of Borax to soften the water and help get rid of soap residue.

# Pre-wash formula for heavily stained clothes

Rub the clothes with pure soap and leave to stand overnight.

— *OR* —

▶ Dissolve 30ml of washing soda in 2.25L of hot water and rub into the stain before washing (Use rubber gloves to protect your skin, washing soda can burn a bit).

## THE **COCA-COLA** TRICK

Coca-Cola has an amazing number of uses, including degreasing engines as well as cleaning clothes. So if your clothes are very greasy add the contents of a can of Coca-Cola to the wash to dissolve the grease. Flat or fizzy, it makes no difference.

If you aren't a Coca-Cola household then try a ¼ cup of bicarb thrown into the load.

# GENERAL SOAKERS FOR SOILED CLOTHES

**BICARB SODA** is a good soaking agent and removes stains effectively but it doesn't have the full effect of the main ingredient used in commercial soakers; and that is sodium percarbonate (sodium carbonate peroxyhydrate).

Sodium percarbonate is a free flowing powder with a high concentration of available oxygen content offering many of the same functional benefits as liquid hydrogen peroxide, which is not surprising because it is a powdered form of hydrogen peroxide.

It dissolves in water rapidly to release oxygen and is a powerful cleaning, bleaching, stain removing and deodorising agent.

It increases the pH value in washing water. This increased pH value reduces the negative charges of dirt and fibre resulting in strengthening the repellence between the two and making it a powerful stain removing agent.

It boasts the following advantages in laundry formulations:

+ It's environmentally friendly
+ It's a powerful stain remover
+ It's used for deodorising and disinfecting
+ It's colour safe and fabric safe
+ It doesn't weaken the strength of fabrics
+ It prevents fabrics from yellowing
+ It's effective in a broad range of water temperatures.

As effective as bicarb is as a soaking agent it's a poor cousin to sodium percarbonate.

It's worth keeping a bag of this magic powder in with your other cleaning agents. It can be bought through selected wholesalers or pool suppliers. It's not cheap but it's a very concentrated agent so you don't need to use much – I look on it as the Rolls Royce of laundry soaking agents. A tiny amount in each soaking bucket works wonders.

Bicarb soda is a good soaking agent and removes stains effectively.

# Cheap diaper soakers

Not many people use cloth diapers anymore, it's a shame because it is a far cheaper alternative to disposable diapers and much better for the environment, and they give us an endless supply of soft polishing cloths when the children are toilet trained.

▶ Here's an easy way to keep cloth diapers snowy white.

▶ Dissolve 50ml of bicarb soda in a bucket of hot water and soak the diapers overnight. Be sure to put a lid firmly on the bucket, you don't want any inquisitive little people to topple head first into the bucket if they decide to explore.

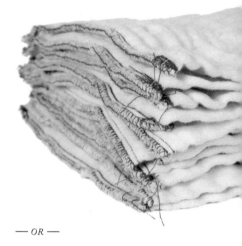

— OR —

▶ Soak the diapers in some of the liquid soap solution (strong mixture) with some white vinegar or eucalyptus oil, which act as a disinfectant and freshener. Use 250ml of white vinegar or a capful of eucalyptus per bucket.

# To remove perspiration stains

It's a shame to have good clothes ruined by perspiration stains but don't despair, there are a few simple solutions.

▶ Dissolve 4 tbsp of salt in 1 litre of hot water. Sponge the stained area, keep sponging until the stain disappears.

— OR —

▶ Try the old shampoo trick to get rid of perspiration or oil stains. Simply rub some shampoo directly onto the stain, leave for a minute or two, rinse and wash as usual. This works well for coloured fabrics, shirt cuffs or collars.

# To remove blood stains from clothing

Soak the affected clothes in cold salted water then wash in warm soapy water. If the stain persists boil them after they have been washed but this is only for natural fibres that can take a high heat.

— OR —

▶ Try liquid hydrogen peroxide or sodium percarbonate, both of these work well but read the washing instructions on the label first, some synthetic fabrics may not handle liquid peroxide very well.

▶ If you are using liquid hydrogen peroxide apply it directly to the stain and wash it as you would normally.

▶ If you are using sodium percarbonate, dissolve a very small amount (as little as ¼ or ½ tsp in a litre or two of water) and soak the garment. Sodium percarbonate is a very strong stain remover; you don't need to use much to get a good result.

# To remove mildew or rust stains

Both of these are extremely hard to remove and it's a matter of *win some, lose some*. It depends on the fabric, how long the stain has been there and whether it has been washed or treated before and has 'set'.

▶ Mix some lemon juice and salt together and moisten the stain. Put the garment out into the sun and get the benefit of the sun's unique bleaching power. Rinse in clean warm water.

— OR —

▶ Spread a paste of cream of tartar and water over the area, leave for a few hours then rinse with warm soapy water.

▶ Unfortunately if the stain has 'set' you'll have difficulty removing it but if you can see some change or some indication that the stain has faded a bit, it's worth giving the garment a second treatment.

# To stop grease from staining clothes

If you spill grease on your clothes and can't wash them straight away, sprinkle the affected area with salt to absorb the grease. All you need do then is scrape the grease soaked salt off your clothes and wash as usual as soon as you have the chance.

# To get oil stains out of silk

Have you ever noticed that even the tiniest crumb of food dropped onto a silk shirt seems to spread a wide oil stain? You have to wonder where all the oil came from. But here is a way to fix the problem.

Gently rub some cornflour into the oil stain for a few seconds then very gently brush the cornflour off to get rid of the surface oil. Cover the stain again with more cornflour and let it sit for about an hour or so. By then the cornflour should have soaked up all the oil on the silk.

Shake the garment to get rid of the powder (don't rub it this time, it will spread the stain) and hand wash or if you are a washing machine person, run it through the gentle cycle on the machine with a soap suitable for silk.

The tiniest crumb of food dropped onto a silk shirt seems to spread a wide oil stain

## TO REMOVE
# WINE
# STAINS FROM
# CLOTHING

Ah, the old red wine on the best shirt disaster. No problem.

1. Get a large bowl and put the clothing over the bowl with the stain in the middle.

2. Cover the stain with salt and let it start to soak up the wine then slowly pour boiling water over the area.

Salt is also a good way to soak red wine spills from your carpet. In fact salt will just about soak up anything given the chance.

# To remove lipstick stains from clothes

If you've had the misfortunate of letting a forgotten tube of lipstick slip through into a wash cycle you're sure to be more than a bit annoyed at the amazing power the lipstick has of staining virtually every item of clothing in the load.

To remove the lipstick spray the affected area with WD40, rinse and rewash.

## Spot cleaning

Eucalyptus oil or glycerine removes persistent stains. Place a few drops on the problem area or soak in a solution of half glycerine/ half water.

**Or**

Dissolve 2 tbsp of bicarb or washing soda in half a bucket of water and leave clothes to soak for an hour. Wash as usual.

**Or**

Try lemon juice and white vinegar, they are both good stain removers.

## Home grown bleach

Lemons are a fantastic bleaching agent, they clean, brighten and have many applications, including lightening age spots on skin. One cup of lemon juice in half a bucket of water is an excellent substitute to soaking in bleach.

## STUBBORN STAINS

If you have a stubborn stain on clothing splash some vodka on the stain and rub it for a while then wash as usual. A dash of vodka usually does the trick.

Lemons are a fantastic bleaching agent

# Fabric softener

To make your own fabric softener mix equal quantities of water, bicarb soda and vinegar in a plastic bottle. Don't fill it right to the top because the bicarb and vinegar will fizz up a bit before settling down.

▶ Keep at hand and add ¼ cup to your wash.

— OR —

▶ Washing soda softens the water and keeps clothes soft. If you're using homemade laundry liquid then the washing soda is already in the detergent and your clothes should come off the line soft and fluffy.

▶ If you are machine washing, dissolve ½ cup of washing soda in hot water and use this as an alternative to commercial softener.

▶ The amount you need will vary according to the hardness of your water supply.

# Ironing fragrance enhancer

The French grannies had a good trick for keeping ladies 'delicates' or 'unmentionables' (as they were called) fresh and delicately perfumed by draping them over a lavender bush to dry in the sun. This is still a wonderful fabric freshener, it's free and the heat of the sun releases lavender perfumes that permeate the garments.

Another way of getting the same result without having to display your underwear on a bush is to mix 85ml (give or take) of 90% proof vodka and 12 drops of lavender oil in an airtight container. Let it sit for a day and then add 350ml of water. Give it a good swish around to mix everything together, transfer the mixture to a spray bottle and store in the fridge ready for use. The lavender scent will keep for about 6 weeks. A fine mist over your 'delicates' will ensure your clothes smell clean and fresh.

# Simple home soaker for handkerchiefs

Not many people use cloth handkerchiefs anymore but for those who do, or live with someone who does, the simple way of getting them clean is to soak them in a salty solution before washing, the salt dissolves the mucous.

# Easy spray-on starch

Dissolve 2 tbsp of cornstarch in 1 litre of water, put into a spray bottle and shake before each use. Adjust the amount of cornstarch used for lighter or stronger starch and if the nozzle of the spray bottle becomes clogged between uses simply soak in hot water for a few seconds to remove any build-up.

If you want to starch delicate fabrics dissolve a small sachet of gelatine (unflavoured) in 2 cups of hot water, test the solution by trying a corner of the fabric, if the fabric dries sticky it means you have too much gelatine – just add more water to the solution.

## ANTI-FREEZE
### (FOR THOSE WHO LIVE IN COLD CLIMATES)

If you live in a cold climate and can't be bothered with defrosting your laundry after hanging it out to dry, throw a handful of salt in the final rinse and you won't have any problems with rock hard frozen laundry.

# To brighten the colour of curtains and rugs

Check the manufacturer's instructions first before washing.

▶ Wash curtains in a strong salt water solution (this brings out the colours in fabrics).

▶ To brighten faded rugs and carpets dip a cloth in a solution of strong salt water, wring it out, wipe over the rug or carpet and you'll be surprised at the result.

Wash curtains in a strong salt water solution to bring out the colours

# To keep fabrics smelling fresh

There are commercial products on the market that help remove odours from clothes or help freshen up curtains and fabrics that can't be washed often but these products can contain a few nasties including cyclodextrin.

You can make a fabric freshener at home that is just as effective, it kills bacteria (which cause odour) by using vodka, which is basically odourless.

Fill an atomizer and spray as required then hang the garment in a gentle breeze if possible. Always spot check a piece of fabric first.

## TO CLEAN
# YOUR IRON

Try as hard as we can something always seems to melt on the base of the iron making it sticky so it doesn't glide easily. I've even excelled in stupidity by melting the plastic resting tray to the iron.

Here's a simple inexpensive trick to keeping the bottom of the iron in good condition.

Put some newspaper on your ironing board, sprinkle it with salt, turn your iron onto a high setting and run the iron over the salt solution to remove the grit.

Always spot check a piece of fabric first

Commercial products can contain a few nasties including cyclodextrin

# bathroom

## KEEP MOULD AND **MILDEW** AT BAY WITH THESE **SIMPLE TIPS**

**WE ALL LOVE** a sparkling bathroom free from the mould and mildew that easily builds up on tiles, grout, shower curtains and screens. Then there's the toilet, commonly called the throne, and blocked drains and plug holes, which are certainly not the most fun cleaning job!

Here are a few recipes that will help get your bathroom glistening again and make it easier to keep clean.

# BATHROOM TILE CLEANER

This is a great cleaner but a word of warning first; *never mix ammonia and bleach as it will give off a toxic gas*. Now we've got that out of the way here we go.

**YOU'LL NEED:**

½ **cup of ammonia**
½ **cup of white vinegar**
¼ **cup of bicarb soda**
**A few drops of citric acid or lemon essential oil (optional)**

1. Mix all the ingredients together in a large pouring jar. The bicarb and vinegar will cause a few bubbles so maybe mix it over the sink.

2. Pour the mixture into a spray bottle and fill to the top with warm water.

3. Spray on your shower tiles and leave for 10-15 minutes then wash off with clean warm water. (I use the handheld shower head to rinse the mixture off tiles around the bath.)

Don't be put off by the smell of the vinegar as it will disappear after a while. The vinegar will stop soap scum building up so go with the flow and you'll be rewarded with an easy to clean bathroom.

## STAINED OR MOULDY TILES

If your tiles are stained or have mould on them you can wash them down with a mixture of diluted bleach. A ratio of 1 part bleach to 2 parts water will work. Wipe the tiles with the bleach mixture, leave for 30 minutes then rinse clean with warm water.

Make sure you have washed the bleach off completely before you use the tile cleaner to finish off the job. You don't want any residue of the bleach on the wall to combine with the ammonia in the tile cleaner.

# KEEPING YOUR GLASS SHOWER SCREEN CLEAN

**GLASS SHOWER SCREENS** look great but they can be a real problem to keep clean. Soap scum can be caused by minerals in hard water or general household soap. Bars of soap can contain talc and it's either minerals or the talc you see building up on the screen.

▶ Changing from bar soap to liquid soap is one way of reducing soap scum build-up, but for those who like to lather up with a bar of soap here are a few tips.

## Simple Spray

Spray with pure vinegar and wipe over with a damp cloth. The vinegar will also help to stop new soap scum forming.

— OR —

▶ Make a mixture of 50% methylated spirits and 50% water. Wipe over with crumpled newspaper. Newspaper leaves an invisible film that stops dirt sticking to the glass.

# Shower squeegee

This doesn't stop you ever having to clean the shower screen but it definitely makes it easier.

▶ Leave a window squeegee in the shower recess and train everyone to run the squeegee down the glass before they get out. It will reduce the soap scum build up and your cleaning will be reduced dramatically.

▶ It's only a matter of getting everyone into the habit and if you leave the squeegee where they'll virtually have to trip over it to get out there's no excuse.

# Stubborn Soap Scum

Sometimes soap scum can be very stubborn – a bit like some people. If you've tried the sprays but find there are some areas of soap build-up that just won't budge use a pad of steel wool (the soaped variety).

▶ Try the lazy man's cleaning method of leaving a mini steel wool pad on the soap tray (in a plastic tray so rust wont stain) for a few days with instructions for everyone having a shower to give the screen a few wipes.

▶ Then when the screen is dazzling you with its sparkling clean glass you'll be able to change over to sprays without any problems.

▶ Different soaps and shampoos seem to leave a different residue and if soap scum is left too long it sets hard, almost like concrete. It can be very hard to remove but don't give up because eventually, like all things in life, it has to fall away.

# Shower screen wipe

Wipe your shower screen with lavender oil to stop soap scum build up.

> If soap scum is left too long it sets hard, almost like concrete

## KEEPING **SHOWER CURTAINS** CLEAN

If you use a shower curtain you'll be plagued with the continual build up of mould, especially along the bottom of the curtain. The easiest way to keep the shower curtain free from mildew is to keep the moisture in the bathroom down to a minimum by making sure the bathroom is aired regularly. Mildew can't form where there is good air circulation.

# To prevent mildew forming

To prevent mildew reforming soak the curtains in a solution of salted water before you hang them. Make it hard for mildew to get a grip on anything by turning the fan on when you're showering to get as much excess moisture out of the bathroom as possible.

▶ While you're drying yourself leave the shower curtain stretched rather than bunched up at one end of the bath. Put the curtain inside the bath while the excess water runs away then move it to outside the bath where there is better air flow to give the curtain a better chance of drying quickly.

▶ Give the curtain a weekly spray with a weak bleach or vinegar solution or hit it with the Listerine trick to kill mildew spores. Listerine is a great way to get rid of bacteria and other nasties but it needs to be the genuine Listerine, the imitation mint mouth washes won't work. Give a light spray, leave for 10 – 15 minutes then give it a quick scrub and rinse clean.

# To remove mildew

If you find the mould build up hard to remove try rubbing bicarb soda before you wash the curtain in hot soapy water and if you hang them straight away the creases will fall out.

▶ I find hand washing much gentler on the curtain than machine washing but if you do throw it into the washing machine make sure you use the delicates cycle.

## To stop bathroom mirrors steaming up

Rub the mirror over with a bar of dry soap then polish with a clean cloth. If you do this regularly you won't have any problem with the mirror steaming.

# CEILINGS FREE FROM MILDEW

Spray a mixture of 50% hydrogen peroxide and 50% water on the bathroom ceiling every 6 months to stop mildew forming.

**Or**

Mix 3 drops of clove oil in 1 litre of water and use to wipe areas where mildew is prone to develop.

## To remove mineral build up around taps

It's not easy to get into the crevices around taps and bath-room fittings to get rid of white mineral build up, however if you dampen a cloth with vinegar and wrap the cloth around the tap, leave it overnight and you'll find the mineral deposits will wash away quite easily the next morning.

## To remove mildew from around sinks

Make a solution of lemon juice and sea salt and rub it into the area. Leave for 10 minutes then wipe off with a damp cloth.

## BLOCKED PLUG HOLES AND **DRAINS**

Pour a salt water solution down your drains regularly; ½ cup of salt to 1 litre of hot water is a good ratio. If they are really blocked, wait for them to be completely dry then pour down 1 cup of bicarb soda followed by 1 cup of vinegar. Wait for the fizzing to stop, pour down 1 cup of boiling water. Repeat if necessary.

## To get rid of hair and shampoo residue from drains

No-one likes having to pull out the mess that hair and shampoo leave in the bathtub drain. Here's an easy solution.

Mix 1 cup of salt with 1 cup of bicarb soda and 1/2 cup white vinegar, pour down the drain then run the hot tap for a few minutes until the drain is clear.

# GENTLE BATH AND TUB CLEANER

## Easy to Use Grout Cleaner

Nothing makes the bathroom look shabbier than stained grout. Here's a simple way to fix the problem.

**YOU'LL NEED:**

½ **cup of vinegar**
½ **cup of borax**
½ **cup of bicarb soda**

Mix everything together – it should resemble a thick paste. Rub the stained grout with an old toothbrush dipped in the paste then rinse with warm water.

— *OR* —

Mix a paste of 2 parts bicarb soda and 2 parts vinegar (or lemon juice); it will fizz up a bit. Apply to the grout with a toothbrush, leave for 10 minutes then rinse with warm water.

**YOU'LL NEED:**

⅓ **cup of borax**
⅓ **cup of bicarb soda**
**Your favourite essential oil (optional)**

Put everything together in a bowl, making sure the essential oils are mixed through. Sprinkle some of the powder onto a damp scourer and start cleaning, it works wonders. Rinse off with warm water.

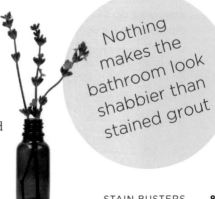

Nothing makes the bathroom look shabbier than stained grout

# THE TOILET

## (OR AS IT'S COMMONLY KNOWN - THE THRONE)

## To clean and disinfect toilets

Pour 2 capfuls of eucalyptus oil down your toilet and 2 tbsp of bicarb soda, leave for a few minutes then scrub with the toilet brush and flush. If you don't have any eucalyptus oil handy you can use vinegar with the same result.

— OR —

▶ Listerine is another good toilet cleaner. Pour half a capful into the bowl and use a toilet brush to give the bowl a good scrub, wait 15 minutes or so before flushing. Listerine will kill the bacteria, remove stains, and it will also protect the brush at the same time.

▶ It's a good idea to take the toilet seat off every so often, take it outside or put it in the bottom of the shower and give it a good hose down; most seats come off and slide back on easily. This gives you a chance to get into the underbelly area.

## To remove scale from the toilet bowl

Pour flat Coca-Cola or Pepsi into the toilet bowl and leave overnight to soak. In the morning give the toilet bowl a good scrub with a firm brush and flush.

— OR —

▶ Make a paste of borax and lemon juice and apply to the sides of the toilet. Leave for a few hours then scrub the surface with a firm brush and rinse.

## Cheap air freshener

Put a few drops of your favourite essential oil on the inside of the toilet roll, where the cardboard tube is. Every time the roll is pulled it will release a pleasant scent.

— OR —

▶ Light a match and let it burn for a few seconds; this is a quick and effective method.

## To freshen the toilet brush

The toilet brush holder will stay fresh if you keep the brush in good condition. Soak it in a solution of bicarb soda regularly and put a few drops of lemon juice or tea tree oil in the bottom of your toilet brush holder as a double whammy.

## To remove odours from your bathroom

Put a small open container filled with bicarb soda in the corner of the room. Change the bicarb every month or so.

— OR —

▶ Another method is to fill a spray bottle with vinegar and water and keep it handy. Spray to freshen up the room. The vinegar smell will disappear and if you want a lingering smell add your favourite essential oil to the bottle.

Put a few drops of your favourite essential oil on the inside of the toilet roll

# personal care

## TAKE CONTROL AND LEARN **NATURAL ALTERNATIVES** THAT WILL **MAKE YOUR BODY GLOW**

**NO CLEANING BOOK** would be complete without a section on cleaning tips to keep ourselves squeaky clean and brimming with the confidence that comes from a healthy, glowing body.

From toothpaste alternatives to natural teeth whiteners and strengtheners, breath fresheners, deodorant, shampoo and even baldness remedies, you don't have to rely on the supermarket shelves to meet your personal care needs.

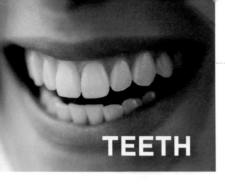

# TEETH

**THERE WAS A TIME** when it was fashionable to have rotten teeth. Hard to imagine but it's true. Only the wealthy could afford refined food and their recipes called for huge amounts of sugar, which naturally rotted their teeth. Social climbers, impatient for the full rotten teeth look, would blacken their teeth to make sure they fitted into high society.

Round about the same time peasants used sticks as toothbrushes. One end of the stick was carefully separated into long slivers creating what best could be described as a mini broom effect.

We've come a long way and our supermarket shelves are stocked to overflowing with various forms of dental care but there are few that can't be duplicated at home at just a fraction of the cost.

Tooth enamel is 96% minerals and the health of our teeth is dependent on the continual process of the de-mineralising and re-mineralising of the enamel. The trick is to make sure we re-mineralise more than we de-mineralise.

# Water and tooth decay

The first line of defence against tooth decay is making sure we have a healthy diet and drink enough water to keep ourselves hydrated. Water is crucial to saliva. Saliva contains calcium and phosphate and acts to cleanse and heal our teeth.

The other way in which water helps prevent tooth decay is as a rinse after you have consumed something acidic (sugary food, soft drinks etc). Rinse then spit the water out and you'll reduce the chances of acid damage, which is the biggest dental problem today.

# Toothbrush

A good toothbrush plays a major role in teeth hygiene and a simple trick to making sure your brush lasts longer is to soak it in salt water before use.

There are few dental care products that can't be duplicated at home at just a fraction of the cost

## TOOTHPASTE

The role of toothpaste is to remove plaque, keep teeth clean and freshen up the breath. So there are 3 functions for us to explore.

## Commercial 'look-a-like' toothpaste

If you like to squeeze your toothpaste from a tube here is a simple and extremely effective homemade product that will leave your teeth so clean and white you'll never be tempted to reach for the commercial paste again.

▶ Simply mix some bicarb soda with a small amount of water to create a paste. Flavour with a few drops of peppermint or spearmint oil.

— OR —

▶ Better still, and particularly if you have a problem with an infected tooth, add a drop or two of either clove oil, tea tree extract or olive leaf extract. These three ingredients are superb for infection and the clove oil will take the pain away. Make your own brand of toothpaste with a little bit of experimentation until you come up with what suits you best.

▶ The mixture will dry out after a while so work with small quantities to keep the paste pliable and make sure the lid is kept on the tube when not in use. You can actually buy 'tubes' from health food shops, they're re-useable and easy to fill, or you can cut the end off your commercial toothpaste, fill with your new improved homemade version and seal.

# Powdered toothpaste

Simply sprinkle bicarb soda on your toothbrush; the taste is rather salty but not unpleasant and if you rinse your mouth afterwards with a solution of water and a few drops of peppermint oil your mouth will be fresh and your teeth plaque free.

▶ If you find sprinkling the powder on the brush too messy then put a small amount of bicarb in the palm of your hand (about the size of a pea) and dip your wet toothbrush into the powder.

# Dentures

If you have false teeth use a solution of bicarb dissolved in water to soak your dentures in to keep them fresh and stain free.

▶ If the dentures are badly stained mix ¼ tsp of citric acid with 1 tsp of bicarb in a glass, pop the dentures in and cover with water. The citric acid and bicarb will bubble and give the dentures a fast and furious clean.

# Berry good toothpaste

Strawberries and raspberries both make excellent alternatives to toothpaste. Cut the berries in half and rub over the teeth or mash them and use as a paste on your toothbrush. Leave the fruit on your teeth for a while then rinse with clean water. Both berries will prevent tartar build-up and they taste so good.

▶ Africans use ripe figs to clean their teeth. Cut the fig in half and rub the cut half over the teeth for a brilliant white smile.

# Tooth soap

There are a number of commercial products on the market, which can be expensive, but you can substitute the commercial tooth soap for a simple alternative by using a natural, olive oil based soap. Run your wet brush across the soap until you have enough on the brush to clean your teeth.

▶ Make sure the soap doesn't have any perfumes, unless they are ones you are happy to brush your teeth with, e.g. peppermint.

▶ Using this method is a simple and quick alternative to oil pulling with olive oil.

# Oil to clean teeth

'Oil pulling' is another effective way to clean your teeth. Swill a teaspoon of olive, sesame or coconut oil around your mouth for a while, about 10 – 15 minutes before spitting it out. You'll find the oil has changed colour to white and your teeth will feel clean.

▶ Oil pulling has the additional benefit of encouraging saliva and releases minerals back into the mouth, which adds to tooth strength.

# TEETH WHITENERS

**IT HAS BECOME** fashionable to have teeth so white people need sunglasses to protect their eyes when you smile but concerns have been raised about the damage some of these processes may cause.

The colour of teeth is determined by extrinsic and intrinsic influences. The extrinsic influences that cause discoloration are poor diet, poor dental hygiene, the use of antibiotics, iron tablets and other substances we put into our mouths.

The intrinsic influences can be genetic or caused by bad dental hygiene. Teeth enamel is a natural pearly white colour over an under-lying layer of a yellow hard tissue called dentin. If the enamel is worn away or damaged the yellow of the dentin can show through and if this is the case no amount of whitening of the enamel will change the situation.

If you are looking for a bright pearly white set of teeth here are a few simple, cheap, effective and problem free alternatives. A word of warning, please be careful and protect your precious teeth enamel from damage caused through overzealous brushing.

If you are using the bicarb soda homemade toothpaste you already have your teeth whitener built in. Bicarb soda is a superb tooth whitener but if you would like variety here are a few others to consider.

▶ Citrus fruits make an excellent teeth whitener. Mix equal parts of grapefruit, lemon and lime juice and use this on your brush three times a week. Make sure you rinse you mouth thoroughly afterwards because citrus juice is extremely acidic and you're not doing your teeth any favours if you leave acid residue in your mouth for any period of time.

▶ If you have yellow stains on your teeth try brushing with black walnut powder. Black walnut powder will also help remove plaque and tartar but is a bit abrasive, so don't use it too often and be gentle when you brush. Tooth enamel may be hard (in fact it's the hardest substance in our body) but it's also delicate and doesn't take too kindly to rough handling.

# Teeth strengtheners

Have you ever wondered why sugar rots your teeth? The body needs calcium to break sugar down and so pulls calcium from the teeth and wherever else it can get it from (including bones) so the sugar can be processed.

Tooth enamel is only 3mm thick; it's the hardest substance in our body and is in a state of constant mineralisation and de-mineralisation. Even the smallest changes to the acidity can create weak spots where bacteria can penetrate.

The road to healthy teeth starts when we are very young. Good diet and good dental hygiene practices learned at an early age help our bodies form strong teeth that will last us a lifetime.

Strengthening and protecting teeth is the best way to avoid tooth decay and cavities. Not everyone is fortunate to have strong healthy teeth and here is a simple method for keeping teeth strong and in good condition regardless of your age.

# Natural strengtheners from nature's cupboard

Include rhubarb in your diet or juice the stalks and use the juice on your brush to protect and strengthen your teeth. Rhubarb has high levels of the mineral salts calcium, potassium and phosphorus, and according to the Eastman Dental Centre in the United Sates, rhubarb juice seems to coat tooth enamel with a protective film.

▶ Another gem from nature's cupboard is the humble date. Dates provide fibre, vitamins, minerals and amino acids but they also provide a rich source of fluorine, and as the name suggests fluorine is a close relative of fluoride but from a natural source. Fluorine helps fight early decay.

# Mouth Wash

This takes a few minutes to make but is well worth the effort.

1. Combine 175ml of water and 60ml of vodka in a saucepan and boil gently for a minute then add 4 tsp of glycerine and 1 tsp of aloe vera gel and simmer for another minute until everything is combined.

2. When the mixture has cooled, add 10 or more (depending on taste) drops of either peppermint or spearmint oil.

3. Give it a good shake, store in an airtight container and use as needed.

Although there is very little alcohol in the vodka, alcohol does dry the mouth and can affect the level of saliva so be sure you rinse your mouth with water after use.

# Breath Fresheners

Commercial mouth washes and breath fresheners contain a high percentage of alcohol, which dries the mouth and inhibits healthy saliva, as well as glycerine, which coats tooth enamel, blocking re-mineralisation.

The best breath freshener is a healthy diet with lots of water but here are a few tricks to keep up your sleeve.

+ **Chew parsley to get rid of garlic breath.**
+ **Make a chewable breath freshener from coffee beans and fresh mint leaves.**
+ **Chew fennel seeds, they will freshen the mouth (and also inhibit appetite).**
+ **Eat yoghurt every day; it helps internal bacteria and sweetens the stomach acting as an effective breath freshener.**
+ **Try a gargle of 1 tsp of honey and 1 tsp of cinnamon powder mixed in hot water, this will keep your mouth fresh throughout the day.**

# Furry Tongue remedy

A lot of toothbrushes have a tongue cleaner attachment which can be difficult to use and produces a similar reaction to sticking your finger down your throat. Not a load of fun first thing in the morning.

▶ Furry tongue can be caused by dehydration and rectified by something as simple as making sure your body is hydrated. Although there are other causes including alcohol consumption and smoking, both of which dehydrate the mouth and reduce saliva. If you enjoy the odd drink (or two) or smoke, make sure you drink plenty of water to keep the saliva in your mouth flowing.

▶ Another quick fix is to gargle 1 tsp of bicarb soda in a glass of water three times a week and it won't be long before you see a marked difference.

▶ For those who want to bring in the heavy guns, or for those with a sense of adventure, this is one to have some fun with. Put some bicarb soda on your tongue, making sure it covers the area where the tongue is coated or furry. Before the bicarb has time to absorb saliva (or you are tempted to swallow) add some apple cider vinegar (you don't need much, a tablespoon will do) then close your mouth quickly and swish the mixture around for as long as you are able to hold it while it fizzes and bubbles before spitting out and rinsing your mouth with water. Your mouth (and breath) will stay fresh for hours.

## QUICK FIX FOR A **FURRY TONGUE**

Combine ¼ tsp of citric acid with 1 tsp of bicarb soda; these ingredients are inert while they are in a dry state but leap into life producing a brilliant amount of carbon dioxide bubbles when water is added.

Put ½ tsp of the mixture over your tongue, especially where there is any coating or build-up of bacteria, take a swig from a glass of water, close your mouth and let the bubbles do their magic.

If you find the salty taste unpleasant add a few drops of peppermint to the water for a fresh mint taste.

# DEODORANTS

**THE CHOICE OF** deodorant is very important. The armpit houses a major lymph gland (clears toxins from the body) and it is very important that this lymph gland is not blocked or loaded with aluminium based products, which can cause health problems.

Sweating is our body's natural air-conditioner or cooling system. It's the body's way to regulate body temperature and antiperspirants may not be the best thing to use because they temporarily block the sweat glands and stop them from doing their work. Better a damp patch of perspiration than a blocked lymph gland.

If you would like to make your own chemical free deodorant here are a few suggestions.

+ Use turnip juice, stored in a plastic squirt bottle, it is easy to use, won't interfere with the sweat glands and keeps the body fresh for around 10 hours.

+ Try the crystal deodorants, they are inexpensive, chemical free and last for ages.
+ Make infusions of the herbs lovage or cleavers, use directly on your underarm or add some to the bath water.
+ Mix cornstarch and bicarb soda together in a ratio of 50-50 and dust your underarms using a powder puff.
+ Try coconut oil. Perspiration is basically water and has no smell; it's bacteria that create the odour. Extra virgin coconut oil has amazing bacteria killing powers and is also good for skin rashes and cuts, to name a few uses. It's easiest to use when cold (as it solidifies). Simply put a small pea size amount onto your armpit and rub in, as it melts it will turn to oil. My husband swears by this and he works outside all day in the heat. He hasn't used a commercial deodorant for ages and I vouch for the fact that I'm more than happy to get up close and personal to those armpits any time.

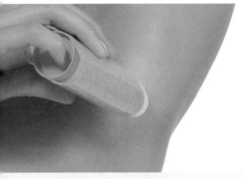

## HOMEMADE
# STICK DEODORANT
## FOR **SENSITIVE SKIN**

Prepare homemade stick deodorant (left) but increase the cornstarch and decrease the bicarb to a ratio of 60% cornstarch to 40% bicarb. Experiment a bit to see what ratio suits you best.

# Homemade stick deodorant

This is a variation of the cornstarch/bicarb powder deodorant held together with coconut oil. An essential oil fragrance can be added if desired.

Mix cornstarch and bicarb soda in a bowl in equal parts then add a small amount of solid coconut oil. Stir until your mixture reaches a stiff consistency.

Using an empty stick deodorant container or some-thing similar, ram the mixture firmly into the container - keep pushing it in until it is packed tightly. Leave it for a few days to set hard. It should roll on without leaving any film, how-ever in extremely hot weather the coconut oil may liquefy, if it does just move the container to a cool place.

# Homemade deodorant spray

Fill a small spray bottle with rubbing alcohol or 95% grain ethyl alcohol and spray under-arms to protect against body odour caused by bacteria. A word of friendly advice; this is not a good deodorant to use if you have just shaved your armpits, it will sting a bit.

## Awesome Hand Cleaner

To get hands clean after finishing a dirty job use a mixture of sunflower oil mixed with sugar (a small quantity of each is sufficient). Rub the mixture into your hands until they're clean then rinse off with warm water. It keeps well so there's no problem in making up a large quantity and storing in a wide mouth plastic container. Keep near the sink for ease of use.

# Emergency shaving cream

Need a shave but don't have any shaving cream left? Try using peanut butter; it gives a good shave and leaves the skin soft. This is a suitable recipe for ladies who shave their legs also.

## QUICK AND EASY
## BARRIER CREAM

This is a great cream but it doesn't keep and you'll need to make it as needed. Simply mix an egg yolk with 1–1½ tablespoons of sunflower oil and enough kaolin* powder to make a paste.

Rub the mixture into your hands before you do any heavy work and it will keep your hands soft and make them easier to clean afterwards.

(Koalin - or china clay - will absorb oil and is an excellent cleanser. It also has an astringent effect and is good for removing impurities from your skin. If you have trouble sourcing it locally you can buy it of the internet.)

## Free liquid soap

Everyone loves a freebie and here's a nice simple way to keep your liquid soap dispenser constantly full.

Put a container somewhere in the bathroom where you can throw all your left over bits of soap, the little bits at the end of the bar that are too small to use. Once you have a reasonable amount of scrappy bits grate and combine them with some glycerine and hot water. The hot water will melt everything down to a nice consistency perfect for your soap dispenser.

# SHAMPOOS

Making your own shampoo is a matter of trial and error

**OUR HAIR IS** our crowning glory and making your own shampoo is a matter of trial and error because everyone's hair is so different; oily, dry, damaged or coloured. Try some of these recipes and adjust them to suit your personal needs. You may need to develop a few different shampoos to accommodate the quirks of each member of the household but once you get your recipe right you'll never be tempted to settle for commercial shampoo again.

Most commercial shampoos and conditioners contain sodium laureth sulfate (SLES) and sodium laluryl sulfate (SLS). These are effective foaming agents, known in the industry as surfactants. Both are irritants and cannot be metabolised by the liver, which means they stay in our body tissues for a long time before our body can get rid of them. They are easily absorbed through the skin and once absorbed mimic oestrogen. They have been linked to a myriad of health problems including female cancers, depleted male fertility, menopausal problems and PMS. It is particularly concerning that it is used in children's bubble bath.

Sodium laureth sulfate and sodium laluryl sulfate are also used in commercial car washers and to degrease engines. Best we avoid both.

Here are a couple of simple shampoo recipes. These home-made products look rather like the commercial ones would look before the sodium laureth sulfate is added and they work just as well for very little or no cost.

# A simple homemade shampoo

The liquid soap mixture you use for the laundry and kitchen is perfect for hair. Mix in a bit of citric acid or bicarb soda (to help break down grease), wash your hair then rinse with lemon or orange juice diluted in water at a ratio of 1 to 10.

# A mild shampoo from the garden

YOU'LL NEED:

50g crushed soapwort root
1 litre of boiling water

Steep the soapwort root in boiling water for 15 minutes. Strain and use the liquid as a milk shampoo. About half a cup per wash should be adequate.

# Egg and Citrus shampoo

YOU'LL NEED:

1 egg yolk
2 tbsp of orange
   or lemon
   juice (*)
1 cup of soapwort
   infusion (as per
   the recipe for
   the mild shampoo)

Beat the egg yolk with the citrus juice and add to the soapwort infusion and use as an all-in-one treatment.

(*) lemon juice will give blond highlights. Orange juice is suitable for all hair shades.

## Simple dandruff treatment

Dandruff can be a sign that the kidneys are sluggish, try a kidney cleanser or drinking lemon and barley water.

▶ For a simple dandruff treatment make a strong infusion of nettles in a cup of cider vinegar. Use this to massage your scalp twice a day until your scalp is dandruff free.

— *OR* —

▶ Rub coconut oil into your scalp, leave for 1 minute then rinse with warm water.

## DRY SHAMPOO

A quick waterless solution to oily hair between washes is to mix equal parts of arrow-root powder with orris root powder, mix well, sprinkle through your hair then rub into the scalp, leave for 10 minutes and brush vigorously to remove the powder.

Your hair will look and feel clean and fresh. A great way to keep hair looking good when camping and water is scarce.

# Baldness

**HAVING COVERED** recipes for those who have hair let's look at recipes for those who don't have or have very little hair.

Hair follicles are small tubes just below the surface of the scalp that hold the oil glands and hair roots in place. Hair is a protein, which is why good diet and protein is so important for healthy hair. Hair is basically made up of dead cells (keratin – a type of protein) and the only part of the hair that is alive is the root.

Let's cut to the chase and get down to the root of the problem. Baldness, or hair thinning, is a fascinating subject. There are ome very expensive (and painful)

treatments for baldness, however it is possible to reverse some types of baldness with a few simple, inexpensive methods.

There are many reasons for baldness; hereditary, dietary, medications, stress, and even excessive intake of animal fats through over indulging in fast foods. Another reason for baldness can simply be clogged ducts blocking the growth of new hair, so when the old hair completes its cycle and falls out the new replacement hair is unable to penetrate the blockage. A nice warm steaming poultice could be just the thing to unplug the blockages and get things back to normal.

> It is possible to reverse some types of baldness with a few simple, inexpensive methods.

# Garlic as a hair restorer

Crush a clove of garlic to release the juice then gently rub the clove and juice evenly over the scalp. Leave for an hour then add some olive oil to the mix and give your scalp a gentle massage with the emphasis on the word gentle – you don't want to damage any new growth by vigorous rubbing.

▶ Leave the mixture on your scalp overnight then shampoo your hair first thing in the morning. We suggest you use a shower cap to protect your bedding while you sleep.

▶ The heat from your body together with the garlic and olive oil will act as a poultice cleaning the scalp and preparing the way for new hair growth.

▶ Garlic also stimulates the flow of blood (which is reduced through stress and other lifestyle issues), provides nourishment to hair follicles and kills off any germs, parasites or fungi that may be damaging the hair follicles and contributing to the hair loss.

# Removing chewing gum from hair

Every parent's nightmare; a combination of hair matted with sticky gum and a whining, wriggling child as you try and pull the gum out. Here's a simple trick to solve the problem. Try rubbing peanut butter on the gum, massage it a bit to work it into the gum and you'll find that you can wipe it off with a cloth.

# Quick onion treatment for hair re-growth

Onions have a very high level of sulphur, in fact the highest levels of sulphur in the body is in hair, skin and nails, hence the reason sulphur is called the 'beauty mineral'. Sulphur helps regenerate hair follicles and is also good to promote shiny hair and strong nails.

▶ Juice a raw onion and apply the juice over the scalp, massaging gently so the juice penetrates into the hair roots. Leave the juice on the scalp for around 30 minutes, barely the time it takes to watch the news on TV, then shampoo.

# Happy hands sugar scrub

## PAMPER PACKS

This recipe came from my little sister who treated us to some of her awesome recipes as Christmas treats.

**THESE AREN'T JUST** great treats for yourself; they make brilliant budget savvy gifts as well. Find an old jar and make up a special label as gifts for friends and family, they'll love you for it.

We all hear how bad sugar is for our insides but it's an absolute treat for our outsides. It's a perfect scrub base, lasts for months, costs only cents, and it will leave you feeling like you have just left a day spa (where they probably use the same basic ingredients listed in the following recipes). I use sugar to get rid of my 'onion hands' when I have been chopping onions or garlic, it leaves my hands feeling incredible!

**YOU WILL NEED:**

2 ½ cups of white sugar
1 cup of oil (I use olive oil
    but coconut oil will give
    you the same results)
2 tbsp of lemon juice
    (or essential oil)
A few pieces of lemon zest
    (not critical but it gives
    the mixture a nice fresh
    smell and helps to get
    those hands really clean)

1. Mix all ingredients together then bottle up and keep near your sink.

2. To use, wash your hands in warm water then scoop out some hand scrub and scrub away.

3. Rinse in warm water and stand back to admire your freshly smelling, totally clean, silky soft hands.

# The ultimate facial scrub

This recipe was passed on by a friend and it's a real winner, once tried you'll never be tempted to buy a commercial face scrub again. The recipe uses nature's best rejuvenating products.

Honey is a natural preserver that rehydrates and retains moisture. Honey is such an amazing product that jars found in pyramids have been aged at over 5000 years and still judged to be perfect, imagine what it can do for your skin!

Olive oil is another of nature's natural moisturisers. When mixed with lemon juice (a natural bleach for age spots and blemishes) and sugar (a base for the scrub to peel away dead skin cells and open up pores) you have a wonderful healthy scrub for your face, neck and shoulders.

**YOU WILL NEED:**

**2 tbsp of honey**
**1 tbsp of lemon juice**
**1 tbsp of olive oil**
**1½ tbsp of white sugar**

Mix all ingredients together and store in an airtight container. (The recipe calls for fresh lemon juice so it's best to make up a new batch each week and keep it in the fridge.)

To use: dampen your face with warm water, apply a small amount of the scrub to your fingertips, and rub into the skin using a circular motion over your face, neck and shoulders. Rinse with warm water then stand back and admire the results.

Use twice a week but not more. Scrubs are great for removing dead skin cells but it isn't a case of 'more is better'. If you over use a scrub there is a chance that you may remove new healthy skin cells as they replace the old spent cells and leave your skin red and irritated.

If you have sensitive skin, try the below recipe without the olive oil and with added bicarb soda.

Scrubs are great for removing dead skin calls but it isn't a case of "more is better"

**YOU WILL NEED:**

2 tbsp of honey
1½ tbsp of lemon juice
1 tbsp of bicarb soda
1½ tbsp of white sugar

Mix the wet ingredients together. In a separate bowl mix the bicarb and white sugar before adding to the wet ingredients, it will foam a bit as the bicarb hits the lemon juice so make sure you have enough head on the bowl to avoid it spilling over. The foam will go away after a few minutes.

To use: dampen your face with warm water, apply a small amount of the mixture to your fingertips, and rub into the skin using a circular motion over your face, neck and shoulders. Rinse with warm water.

# Elbow Scrub with vanilla and brown sugar

This one is really good for rough heels and elbows, as an exfoliate for your legs and even as a preparation to remove or prepare for fake tans. It will last for months so there's no problem making up big batches.

**YOU WILL NEED:**

2 cups of brown sugar
1 cup of white sugar
1 cup of oil (I use olive oil but if you prefer you can use almond, walnut, sunflower or coconut)
1 tbsp of vanilla paste (you can use extract but you won't get the full vanilla impact)

1. Run your fingers through the sugar to remove any lumps then add your oil and the vanilla paste.

2. Mix everything together thoroughly, bottle and seal.

3. To use, simply wet the area you want to treat, apply a small amount of the scrub and massage into your skin in a circular motion.

4. Rinse with warm water, although it's so natural and smells so good you could almost lick it off.

# MOISTURISERS

**NOW THAT ALL** the dead cells have been removed and your skin is glowing with healthy radiance it's time to look at moisturisers. Don't reach for overpriced, chemical laden varieties; here are some natural, easy, inexpensive ways to moisturise your skin.

## Coconut Oil

For those of you who haven't had the opportunity to discover the amazing capacity of coconut oil and all its wonders then you are about to be surprised. Coconut oil to the body is what bicarb is to the cupboard. It literally has thousands of uses. You can buy it at any health food shop or local farmer's market and it lasts for months on the shelf, but you have to make sure that you buy the pure 100% coconut oil.

For an easy (and I do mean easy) face moisturiser just apply a small amount of coconut oil to your face and rub in, it may feel greasy but it will be absorbed and leave your skin smooth and hydrated.

Transfer the coconut oil into a handy container for the bathroom, an old pump pack bottle from a previous moisturiser would be ideal.

If straight coconut oil sounds a little too simple to be true don't be fooled, it is one of nature's miracle oils. Coconut oil works wonders for dry and damaged skin, cuts, bruises, and speeds up healing while fighting infection. Coconut oil forms a protective barrier to hold in moisture and also penetrates into the deeper layers of the skin to help keep connective tissues strong and supple. Coconut oil is readily absorbed into the skin, helping to reduce the appearance of fine lines and wrinkles. It aids in exfoliating the outer layers of dead skin cells, making the skin smoother. Coconut oil is used to treat dry and damaged hair and as a lathering ingredient for natural shampoos and soaps. It also has wonderful antibacterial qualities and can be used as a cream for eczema, rashes and thrush. It's a perfect all-in-one product for men, can be used as a hair gel, shaving cream, deodorant, conditioner, moisturiser and sunburn cream. It will congeal when it cools so you can leave it in the fridge or in your cupboard (it's easier to use when it's cold).

Coconut oil is also fantastic for your insides (and if they are healthy your outsides look much better). There are numerous claims that adding coconut oil to your diet increases energy, balances hormones, and stimulates the thyroid gland. The cholesterol-lowering properties of coconut oil are linked directly to this ability to stimulate thyroid function. Coconut oil raises your metabolic rate, helping to release energy and promote weight loss. Researchers believe that coconut oil is different from other saturated fats because it is composed of medium-chain fatty acids.

Convinced? Hard not to be.

Adding coconut oil to your diet increases energy and balances hormones

# Body mask

Try mixing the healing qualities of honey with the hydrating qualities of coconut oil for one of the loveliest body masks imaginable.

**YOU WILL NEED:**

**Some towels**
**1 tbsp of raw honey**
**2 tbsp of coconut oil**
**A few drops of your favourite essential oil.**

1. Mix everything together in a bowl and prepare yourself for a real treat.

2. Wet the towels in warm to hot water and wring out the excess water so the towels are moist but not dripping.

3. Make yourself comfortable, perhaps in the bath or somewhere where you feel relaxed and safe from interruptions.

4. Smear your body with the body mask mixture and cover yourself with the warm moist towels.

5. Let your mind wander and your body relax as you soak up the warmth and healing qualities of this amazing mixture.

6. When the towels are cool it's time to wipe your body clean, removing all traces of the body mask. Your skin will feel as soft as a baby's.

# Eye Cream

No need to buy expensive eye creams, the easiest and most efficient method has been a close kept secret for years. But now the secret's out - simply buy Vitamin E capsules and squeeze a small amount out of a capsule each night.

You don't need much and you'll be surprised at how far a small amount goes. Use a pin to prick a hole in a capsule to avoid wastage.

The skin around the eye is of a finer texture than skin on the rest of your face or body. Vitamin E is the perfect oil for this sensitive area.

# Simple facial pamper treatment – exfoliate and rejuvenate

Grapes are nature's little balls bouncing with antioxidant packed compounds and are a perfect way to rejuvenate your skin.

▶ Use crushed grape seeds to exfoliate your skin and grape juice as a wash to help keep aging skin from sagging. The polyphenols in grape juice keep the skin flexible.

▶ But don't stop there; when you've given your face a good wash over with grape juice don't forget to pamper your whole body by drinking a good sized glassful. New research has shown that the beneficial effects of grapes reduce aging damage caused by sunlight and pollution.

# AROMATHERAPY

**AROMATHERAPY IS A** branch of herbal medicine that involves the use of fragrant plant oils called *essential oils* to promote physical and emotional well-being. The use of plant essential oils dates back to ancient times in Egypt, Italy, India and China. French chemist Rene-Maurice Gattefosse coined the term *aromatherapy* in 1937 when he witnessed first-hand the healing power of lavender oil on healing skin burns. Today, aromatherapy is widely practiced and is often integrated into holistic treatments and is used as part of a spa regimen in products such as candles, massage oil, and other relaxation and detoxification materials.

The essential oils used in aromatherapy are *plant volatile oils* from flowers, leaves, stems, buds, branches, or roots that have been extracted using steam distillation, water distillation, cold-pressing (expression), or extraction – which is used on plants too delicate for other methods. The term *volatile* refers to an oil's rapid evaporation rate. Note that essential oils are different from *fixed* or *fatty* oils such as olive oil, which do not evaporate and are consumed for their fatty acids, which provide a multitude of health benefits. And please remember that consumption of undiluted essential oils can be highly toxic.

Essential oils are typically inhaled. They can be used alone or in blends, added to baths, diluted in a carrier oil, or used as massage oils. When inhaled, the scent molecules are thought to travel inside the nose where they stimulate olfactory nerves and eventually parts of the brain that result in a variety of physiological and psychological effects. Essential oils are available in small vials in health food stores, some grocery stores, and online. They can also be found in commercial products such as soaps, lotions, bath salts and candles.

Although it is possible to create your own essential oils with the proper equipment, for the purposes of this book we will be concentrating on pre-made essential oils that you can incorporate into your housekeeping and wellbeing regimens. We recommend looking into specific titles on the subject of aromatherapy if you would like to try your hand at essential oil extraction.

**\*Please note: the ideas presented in this section are meant as a supplement, not a substitute, for professional medical care or treatment.**

# Widely Used Essential Oils and Herbs

## Bergamot

**Primary characteristics:** Sweet, fresh, citrus, light, spicy, refreshing, uplifting, calming, soothing.

**Uses:** Sore throat, bad breath, flatulence, lack of appetite, cold and flu, anxiety, depression, stress.

## Blue Gum Eucalyptus

(also refer to section on Eucalyptus on page 27)

**Primary characteristics:** Woodsy, penetrating, fresh, stimulating, clearing, purifying.

**Uses:** Burns, blisters, cuts, insect bites, muscle aches, circulation, asthma, bronchitis, cough, sinusitis, cold and flu, headache.

## Chamomile

**Primary characteristics:** Fruity, fresh, warm, herbaceous, calming, balancing, relaxing, soothing.

**Uses:** Inflammation, insect bites, sensitive skin, muscle pain, rheumatism, dyspepsia, menstrual cramps, headache, insomnia, migraine, tension, stress.

## Cinnamon leaf

**Primary characteristics:**
Sweet, spicy, peppery, powerful, warming, reviving, strengthening.

**Uses:** Tooth and gum care, warts, stings, colitis, dyspepsia, cold and flu, stress, nervousness.

## Clary Sage

**Primary characteristics:**
Musky, mellow, sweet, relaxing, balancing, inspiring, revitalising, intoxicating, warming.

**Uses:** Acne, dandruff, hair loss, oily skin and hair, muscle aches, asthma, cramps, dyspepsia, flatulence, migraine, depression, tension, stress.

## Clove

**Primary characteristics:**
Hot, floral, fruity, peppery, sweet, spicy, stimulating, warming, comforting, purifying, intense.

**Uses:** Toothache, bruising, cuts, wounds, asthma, bronchitis, dyspepsia, nausea, cold and flu.

## Jasmine

**Primary characteristics:**
Rich, floral, sweet, exotic, uplifting, balancing, warming.

**Uses:** Sensitive skin, muscle spasm, cough, depression, stress, nervousness.

## Lavender

**Primary characteristics:**
Light, floral, mellow, soothing, calming, purifying.

**Uses:** Acne, allergies, inflammation, insect bites, sunburn, bad breath, nausea, depression, insomnia, stress.

## Patchouli

**Primary characteristics:**
Fresh, penetrating, woodsy, strong, stimulating, restorative, purifying, reviving, refreshing.

**Uses:** Hair and scalp conditions, asthma, bronchitis, dyspepsia, flatulence, cold and flu, headache, stress, nervousness.

## Peppermint

**Primary characteristics:**
Fresh, bright, clean, restorative, mental stimulant.

**Uses:** Acne, toothache, sinusitis, cramps, flatulence, nausea, headache, stress, bad breath.

## Rosemary

**Primary characteristics:**
Fresh, woodsy, strong, stimulating, restorative, reviving, purifying.

**Uses:** Acne, eczema, hair and scalp, circulation, rheumatism, colitis, dyspepsia, infection, headache, stress, nervousness.

## Rose Geranium

**Primary characteristics:**
Floral, fresh, powerful, uplifting, soothing, balancing.

**Uses:** Acne, burns, cuts, eczema, circulation, menopausal issues, stress, nervousness.

## Sandalwood

**Primary characteristics:**
Woody, amber, musky, oriental, sensual, masculine, warm, soothing, uplifting, purifying.

**Uses:** Irritated skin, moisturiser, bronchitis, cough, sore throat, nausea, depression, insomnia, tension, stress.

## Spanish Sage

**Primary characteristics:**
Fresh, herbaceous, powerful, refreshing, clearing, invigorating.

**Uses:** Acne, dandruff, hair loss, sores, excessive sweating, arthritis, muscle aches, asthma, cough, cold and flu, headache, stress, nervousness.

## Sweet Orange

**Primary characteristics:**
Warm, sensual, radiant, fresh, citrus, uplifting, soothing, sedative.

**Uses:** Dull complexion, obesity, water retention, cold and flu, constipation, dyspepsia, stress, nervousness.

## Tea Tree
(also refer to section on Tea Tree Oil on page 24)

**Primary characteristics:**
Fresh, powerful, pungent, penetrating, stimulating, refreshing.

**Uses:** Acne, athlete's foot, blisters, burns, bruises, dandruff, insect bites, oily skin, asthma, bronchitis, cough, sinusitis, cold and flu.

# BASIC LAVENDER WATER

250g fresh or 300g dried
    lavender flowers
Sheer cloth bag
    or cheesecloth
Glass container that can
    withstand boiling water
500ml boiling water
Plastic or glass spray bottle

Place the lavender flowers in the cloth bag or tie them in the cheesecloth and place the bundle in the glass container. Pour the boiling water over the bundle and cover the container. After the water cools, remove the lavender bundle, squeezing out all the water. Using a clean piece of cheesecloth or a coffee filter, strain the contents of the glass container. Pour the pure lavender water into the spray bottle and store in a cool, dark place.

Aromatherapy is widely practiced and is often integrated into holistic treatments

# For Household Use

+ **Ironing water** – Please note that while some store-bought ironing waters are safe to pour into you iron's steaming element, homemade ironing water is for spraying directly onto the clothing articles to be ironed.

In a sterilised glass bottle with a tight-fitting lid or cap, mix 360ml of purified (distilled) water with 90ml of 90-proof vodka*. Add 10-15 drops of your favourite essential oil or combination of oils. Cap the bottle and shake the mixture well. Let it stand for 24 hours. Pour the ironing water into a spray bottle and you're ready to go. Store it in the refrigerator for future use.

+ Room spray – Making your own air freshening spray is simple. Use small 120ml bottles and keep one in each room of your house containing your favourite scent combination for that room.

Combine 50ml of distilled water with 50ml 90-proof vodka* and

30-40 drops of your chosen essential oil or combination of oils. Shake well and allow the mixture to sit for several hours. This will help the ingredients incorporate. Spray in your room whenever you feel the urge.

*The alcohol in these recipes helps the scent linger for a longer duration.

+ **Vaporiser** – Vaporisers (or diffusers or humidifiers) are used to distribute vaporised water and essential oils through the air. The vapour can be inhaled for health purposes such as soothing a cough, clearing phlegm, and calming allergies. Camphor-based additives stimulate nerve endings that relieve the symptoms of pain and itching. Menthol, abundant in peppermint oil, helps to clear the respiratory tract. Rosemary is helpful in treating bronchial asthma. And eucalyptus is widely recognised as a decongestant, expectorant, and room disinfectant.

# For Personal Use

+ Homemade hand cream –
In a heavy pot or double
boiler, melt together 60ml
beeswax and 30ml Shea
Butter. When melted,
remove the mixture from
the heat and add 120ml
evening primrose oil and
10 drops of lavender
essential oil (or an essential
oil of your choosing).
Pour the contents into
a sterilised jar with a secure
lid. Let the mixture harden
and the hand softening begin!

+ Facial steam bath – This is
a wonderful non-invasive way
to unclog your pores. Add
5-15 drops of essential oils
to a bowl of hot water. Drape
a towel over your head so that
the ends hang down below
the sides of your face and
slightly over your forehead to
form a barrier for the steam.
Lower your face into the
steam, adding an additional
one or two drops of oil every
five minutes for no more than
15 minutes.

+ Hair care – Use 8ml of
essential oil combined with
500ml of quality shampoo
or conditioner as a hair or
scalp remedy.

Dry hair – cedar wood
**Hair loss – juniper, lavender,
rosemary or sage**
Oily hair – lemongrass
or rosemary
**Dandruff – tea tree oil**

Use 8ml of essential oil combined with 500ml of quality shampoo or conditioner as a hair or scalp remedy

# A Few Suggestions for Inhalation Mixtures

**COMBINATIONS OF THE** oils above, along with other essential oils, can produce a variety of aromatic remedies. Follow the instructions on each bottle of essential oil to create the proper dilution of oil in water.

**Respiratory Health:**
Eucalyptus, Lavender, Peppermint

**Anti-anxiety:** Bergamot, Clary Sage, Jasmine, Lemon

**Irritability:** Sandalwood, Chamomile

**Relaxation and Sleep:** Lavender and Clary Sage

**Insomnia:** Chamomile, Clary Sage, Bergamot

**Headache Relief:** Peppermint, Lavender, Chamomile

**Energising:** Rose Geranium, Rosewood, Rosemary

**Relaxation of Tissues, Muscles and Joints:** Lavender, Tangerine, Marjoram, Chamomile

**Alertness and Mental Acuity:** Ginger, Rosemary, Lemon, Peppermint

**Stress Relief 1:** Cedar, Spruce, Clary Sage, Pine, Ylang Ylang

**Stress Relief 2:** Clary Sage, Lemon, Lavender

**Stress Relief 3:** Jasmine, Grapefruit, Ylang Ylang

**Depression 1:** Bergamot, Clary Sage

**Depression 2:** Jasmine, Lemon, Frankincense

**Depression 3:** Lavender, Ylang Ylang, Grapefruit

# Introducing Others to Natural Products

**ONCE THE MONEY-SAVING** and effective recipes and tricks in this book have taken hold of you, you might understandably want to preach their word with all the fervour and zeal of a religious convert who has seen the natural cleaning light. Chances are that approach will go over like a lead balloon. Instead, try some more subtle ways to introduce others to the fiscal and environmental benefits of being your own cleaning product factory. Take your cue from the suggestions below, and by all means, come up with many more on your own! Hopefully your generosity will spark a chain of giving that inspires more people to clean the natural way.

**Housewarming/welcome wagon:** If you have a new family in the neighbourhood, or if friends are throwing a housewarming, a basket of natural cleaning products makes for a welcome and useful gift to celebrate their move and will go a long way to help them get situated in their new home, where there will be plenty to clean before they've even lived in it a day.

**Raffle prize at a local religious or social organisation function:** Raffle tickets are a great way for organisations to raise a little extra money during social functions. If you'd like to donate to the prize pool but are a bit strapped, people will appreciate the time and talent you put into a selection of homemade products like laundry sprays and essential oil atomisers.

**Hostess (or Host) Party:**
The "Tupperware party" has returned in many forms – from jewellery and makeup to bags and bins. Side businesses are a great way to make a little extra money when in an economic crunch and offer a wonderful excuse to socialise on a weeknight. If you will be hosting a shopping party, as a token of thanks, why not send your guests home with a little "goodie bottle"? They'll appreciate the gesture of gratitude and hospitality and might become repeat customers.

**Secret Santa:** Does your co-worker or third cousin twice removed really need another novelty mug or hideous holiday sweater? Break the cycle of bad compulsory gift giving next holiday season and instead present them with a tasteful collection of homemade hand creams or room sprays and laundry fresheners. The lucky recipient you drew in the lottery will be knocking on your office door and ringing your phone come January for the recipes.

**Shameless Plug:** Place a note card in with your bundle or tie a tag around your atomiser explaining where you obtained the formulas for the products you gift or donate. Or, if you're feeling extra generous, include a copy of *Stain Busters* in the bundle or as a door prize so that they can benefit from all the formulas in this book.

# General Cleaning

## KEEP THESE **GENERAL TIPS** HANDY FOR THOSE NOT-SO-COMMON **CLEANING JOBS**

**THESE GENERAL** cleaning gems provide simple, green advice on the not-so-everyday cleaning needs around your house; from windows to pet hair, removing wine stains from carpet, scratches from wood and giving you smart ideas on how to clean your silverware.

There's also a handful of air freshener options to keep your home smelling fresh using natural ingredients that are safe for your family and pets. Sometimes all a room needs is a little spritz of freshener and an airing out.

## NO STREAK WINDOW CLEANER

Forget the fancy, highly perfumed and toxic commercial glass cleaners; nothing beats the old fashioned methods. You can have windows glistening like diamonds with a few basic household ingredients.

**YOU'LL NEED:**

¼ cup of white vinegar
1 tbsp of cornflour
1 litre of warm water

Put all the ingredients into a spray bottle, give it a good shake to make sure everything is combined, spray onto the area to be cleaned and wipe off with crumpled newspaper or paper towel.

Some newspapers don't work as a wipe for windows because the printers have changed the ink.

*— OR —*

For a simpler method mix 1 tablespoon of cornstarch in 1 litre of warm water in a spray bottle. Spray and wipe. You'll need to rub a bit more if the vinegar is not added but the results will be just as good.

# GENERAL
# WINDOW
# CLEANERS

Mix 2 tbsp of borax in 3 cups of water, spray and rub with dry newspaper.

**Or**

Clean windows with methylated spirits and dry newspaper.
You can use paper towel to dry the glass but newspaper leaves a film that keeps the window clean and streak free – squeaky clean, you'll actually hear the squeak as the paper runs across the glass.

# To remove carpet stains

Red wine can be removed by rubbing either bicarb soda or salt on the stain, both are excellent absorbers.
Soak up as much of the wine as possible by pressing with a paper towel or cloth (anything absorbent – the shirt of the person who spilled the wine would be perfect!). Cover with either bicarb soda or salt, leave for a while until the remaining wine has been absorbed, leave until dry then vacuum.
If the spill is substantial you may need two applications of the bicarb or salt before vacuuming. Wait until the bicarb or salt has absorbed as much of the wine as it can, scrape the mess off using a knife or spoon, then finish the process.

# Foaming Carpet Cleaner

**YOU'LL NEED:**

**¼ cup of liquid soap**
**3 tbsp water**

Whip the ingredients in a bowl with a beater until it foams then rub the foam into the carpet and rinse with water. Always test a corner before attacking the main part of the carpet.

# HERBAL CARPET FRESHENER

Bicarb soda is a superb stain remover and deodoriser, mix it with some essential oils and you have a perfect powder to freshen your carpet. Store in a large jar and if you leave the jar sitting in the corner you have a room freshener as well.

Mix and match to suit your needs but here are a few suggestions to start with.

**YOU'LL NEED:**

**1 cup of bicarb soda**
**½ cup of lavender flowers**

1. Crush the lavender flowers to release their scent before placing in the bicarb soda and putting into a large jar.

2. Shake vigorously to distribute the lavender scent.

3. Sprinkle the powder over the carpet, leave for 15 minutes and vacuum.

— OR —

1. Mix 4 cups of bicarb soda with 35 drops of eucalyptus oil and 30 drops of lavender oil (any combination is fine, this is just a guide).

2. Mix everything together in a bowl, breaking up any chunks that form and store in a large jar.

3. Sprinkle on the carpet, leave for 15 minutes before vacuuming.

# To remove animal hair from carpet and furnishings

We all love to drag our furry friends up onto our laps for cuddle time but the hair left behind (especially in moulting season) is no joy at all.

▶ A quick and easy way to get cat and dog hair out of fabrics or carpets is to rub the area with dampened rubber gloves. A gentle pat with the rubber glove treatment will keep your pets free from loose hair.

# To remove indentations in wool carpets

Put a cloth (a tea towel is perfect) over the indentation to protect the carpet then press with a warm iron. The heat from the iron will get the fibres standing up like a line of little soldiers but don't use this trick on any carpet with synthetics in it, it will melt the fibres and you'll have a patch that looks like dead soldiers on the battle field.

## Floor Cleaner

Add white vinegar into the rinse water after you've washed your floors, the vinegar will help stop dirt or grease sticking to the floor (great for kitchen floors) and if you're into polishing your floors try using a bit of skim milk on the floor (after the floor has dried), it will polish to a beautiful shine.

## To hide scratches on your wood furniture

Take the meat of a walnut (the part we eat) and cut it in half. Rub the soft inside part of the nut over the scratches, this works like walnut oil but you need to use whole fresh nuts you have cracked to get the best results. Most walnuts on the supermarket shelves are quite old and they don't have the same level of fresh oil, but in a pinch they would do if you can't get your hands on the whole nut.

### TO HIDE SCRATCHES ON CERAMIC AND MARBLE FLOORS

Spray with WD40 and the marks will disappear.

Rub the soft inside part of the nut over the scratches

# To remove watermarks on wood furniture

Rub the affected area with toothpaste. Toothpaste is also good for cleaning silver.

# Furniture polish for wood furniture

Mix olive oil and lemon juice at a ratio of 2:1. Gently rub the mixture over the wood, let stand for several hours then polish with a soft cloth.

— *OR* —

▶ Mix the juice of 1 lemon with 1 tsp of olive oil and 1 tsp of water. Pour onto a soft cloth, apply a thin coat to your wood surfaces, leave for 5 minutes and use a clean soft cloth to buff it off. This is best made fresh for each use.

## TO REMOVE
# CRAYON MARKS FROM WALLS

If darling little Johnny has discovered the joy of scribbling on your walls with crayon just spray the area with WD40 and wipe with a clean rag. Works wonders.

# Marble

Marble is porous and can stain very easily. To protect a marble surface from staining polish it with a clear car polish, it leaves a thin film for protection.

# Air fresheners

The commercial air fresheners are designed to cover-up smells, one layer on another.

The best way to keep a house smelling clean and fresh is to open the windows regularly to give the house a good airing but if you like a slight fragrance throughout the house trying simmering some cinnamon sticks, orange peel and a few cloves in water, strain, and spray where needed. A word of warning: check that the spray won't stain or damage areas like carpets, curtains etc.

**Or**

Collect rose petals that have a strong fragrance. Layer the petals with salt in an attractive jar with a tight-fitting lid. Take the lid off when you want to freshen up the room. Seal in between uses.

**Or**

Use a cotton swab to apply a drop of your favourite essential oil on a light bulb, when you turn your lights on the heat from the bulb will fill the room with a lovely fragrance.

**Or**

Mix water and vinegar in a 1:1 ratio, add 10 drops of lavender oil, store in a squirt bottle and spray as needed.

# SIMPLE METAL CLEANERS

## Silver

### Non toxic silver cleaner

All metals (with the exception of gold) rust or corrode with exposure to oxygen through a process that involves electrons moving between the metal and oxygen atoms. It's a pretty spontaneous reaction and silver tarnish is only different because of the combination of sulphur rather than oxygen. It's a bit more of a complex reaction but the principle that tarnishes silver is the same that rusts iron.

The salt water-aluminium trick is the result of a simple chemical reaction called 'ion exchange' whereby the tarnish on the silver is transferred to the foil with the salt water acting as the conductor.

And, if you are cleaning silver that is heavily tarnished you'll be able to see the brown tarnish that has jumped across to the foil. Neat trick hey?

1. Rustle up some tarnished silver.

2. Take some aluminium foil and fold it a few times to make a square mat (shiny side facing outwards).

3. Put the foil into a bowl of warm salted water.

4. Immerse your silver and leave for a while.

5. Remove, dry with a soft cloth.

And you guessed it - perfectly cleaned silver with no rubbing, no polishing, and no nasty chemicals. All for the princely sum of 1 cent worth of aluminium foil and a little bit of salt.

*— OR —*

▶ Use toothpaste, an old soft bristled toothbrush and water. Pretend you are brushing your teeth. The toothpaste will do a brilliant job of cleaning the silver; it's gentle on the silverware and if you make sure you use a soft bristled brush there is no risk of damage or scratching.

*— OR —*

▶ Rub with a paste of bicarb soda and water, rinse then dry with a soft cloth.

# Brass

Mix equal parts salt and flour with a small amount of vinegar, rub the mixture on the brass then buff clean with a dry soft cloth.

# Chrome

Rub with undiluted white vinegar then polish with a soft dry cloth.

# Copper

Rub with lemon juice and salt; or hot vinegar and salt. Either one will work. Rub with a dry soft cloth.

# Stainless Steel

Rub with a paste of baking soda and water, rinse, buff with a dry soft cloth.

## REMOVING
## RUST STAINS

Because rust is formed through corrosion it is extremely hard to get rid of but that doesn't mean it's not worth trying. Here is one way you can attack the problem, and once the rust is removed make sure you seal the area otherwise the cycle will start again as the oxygen begins a new corrosion activity.

Scrub with a stiff or metal brush making sure you remove all traces of rust then cover the area with a sealant.

Rust can only survive where there is oxygen (which is why items at the bottom of the ocean can stay rust free for generations); starve the area of oxygen and you won't have any further problems.

> Because rust is formed through corrosion it is extremely hard to get rid of

## WHY DOES **NEWSPAPER** CLEAN **SO WELL?**

Unlike higher quality paper, newsprint contains no solid components like calcium carbonate or silica, which can scratch glass. Newsprint also leaves minimal lint behind because its individual fibres are more rigid and will not separate as easily as they would from a paper towel, which is more flexible. Additionally, highly polished glass is not absorbent; it actually repels water, whereas newsprint is highly absorbent. When you spray glass cleaner onto a mirror or window, the dirt on the glass clings to the liquid glass cleaner, which is absorbed by the newsprint, and voila! Spotless, scratch-free windows and mirrors!

But take note, while the ink from newsprint will not rub off on glass, it will most likely stain your hands and fingers, so wear rubber gloves if this is a concern.

# What is the gunk on my faucets?

That "gunk" that you might find on the end of your sink faucet and shower head is most likely caused by what's called *hard water*. Hard water is simply water that has a high mineral content, usually calcium, magnesium, lime or even iron. Although it's not harmful to drink, the mineral content in hard water can adversely affect plumbing and can diminish the effectiveness of soap by producing more soap scum than lather. If you've ever wondered why no matter how much you rinse, you can never eliminate the residue of soap from your hands or shampoo from your hair, or why no matter how regularly you clean them, your shower doors always seem dirty, hard water is the most likely culprit! Follow the tips in the "Bathroom" section of this book to combat soap scum and mineral build up in your plumbing and bath area.

# To make candles last longer

Some candles these days seem to go up in smoke in a matter of minutes. To make them last longer seal them in a plastic bag, or wrap them in glad wrap, and leave them in the freezer overnight.

# Make candles drip free

Don't waste money on expensive dripless candles. Buy the el-cheapo candles and soak them in a solution of equal parts water and salt for a few hours, remove, let dry before you light them and they'll burn as usual but won't drip candle wax.

# Removing glue from hands

For the home handyman who is a bit careless with super glue try rubbing some peanut butter into the area then wipe it off with a cloth. Simple but works wonders.

# To remove residue from stickers or duct tape

Wipe with tea-tree oil, eucalyptus or WD40. WD40 is the most effective to remove duct tape residue.

# Can "hard water" affect appliances?

**YES.** The minerals from hard water bond to the elements in appliances that use water, hampering their function. This hardening is called *calcification*. Over time, you may notice white deposits coming through the holes in the soleplate (or face plate) of your iron, or the coffee you brew each morning might begin to take on an unpleasant taste or take noticeably longer to brew. Once again – blame hard water!

To keep your coffee tasting delicious, periodically fill the reservoir of your brewer half way with vinegar and run the coffee maker as normal (without coffee, of course). The vinegar will act as a decalcifying agent that removes the build-up. Then, fill the reservoir full of water and run it again to remove any trace of vinegar. Depending on how often you brew coffee and how hard your tap water is, you may need to perform this *decalcification* as often as once a month.

To prevent further white deposits from forming on your iron, first, clean the soleplate with a paste of vinegar and baking soda to remove any dirt, and wipe it clean. Then repeat the same steps as recommended for the coffee maker, only with a combination of vinegar and water, allowing the liquid to steam for several minutes. Once you unplug the iron, make sure to pour out any unused liquid.

To keep the iron deposit-free, run distilled water rather than tap water through its steaming element during subsequent use, making sure after each use to pour out the unused water once you've unplugged the iron. Distilled water is simply water that has been purified by boiling the water into vapour so that its impurities are left behind and then condensing the vapour into a clean container, a process called – you guessed it – *distillation*. If you use water without impurities in your steam iron, white spots on the soleplate should become a thing of the past in no time.

## Uses for Distillation

Distillation is a common method for separating mixtures based on differences in the conditions required to change the phase (gas, liquid, solid) of components of the mixture. To separate a mixture of liquids, the liquid can be heated to force components, which have different boiling points, into the gas phase. The gas (or vapour) is then condensed back into liquid form and collected.

Distillation is used for many commercial processes, such as production of gasoline, distilled water, xylene, alcohol, paraffin, kerosene, and many other liquids. Types of distillation include simple distillation (described above), fractional distillation, and destructive distillation.

Distillation is also the process used to extract the essential oils found in cleaning, beauty, and aromatherapy products from plants. The simplest method for this is water distillation. The plant material is immersed in water and boiled. The steam and the essential oils rise out of the hot water and are then cooled where they condense and are collected. Two products are created here - the essential oil and the condensed water, which contains water soluble essences of the plant material. These floral waters are called hydrosols. This method works well with flower blossoms and finely powdered plant material.

Steam distillation, the most common method of extracting essential oils, uses a very similar setup to water distillation, except instead of the plant being immersed in the hot water, steam is passed directly through the plant material. The steam breaks open the cells containing the essential oil, and the steam and oil then pass into the cooling chamber where, like with water distillation, two products are created - essential oil and hydrosol.

If you are so inclined, it is possible to create a distillation still at home for the purpose of extracting essential oils from plants.

If you are so inclined, it is possible to create a distillation still at home for the purpose of extracting essential oils from plants

# SALT TRIVIA

+ Epsom salt is not the same as sea salt or table salt. Epsom salt doesn't contain sodium; it is a naturally occurring mineral compound called magnesium sulphate.

+ The United States and China combine to produce 40% of the world's salt supply.

+ More than 200 million tons of salt are used each year. Nearly 300million tons of salt are produced globally each year.

+ Salt preservation is a practice that dates back to the time before written records and was widely used to keep meat, fish and vegetables.

+ Salt was so valuable a commodity that in ancient Roman times, a soldier's pay was called *salarium*, derived from the word *sal* or salt. The word *salary* is derived from the Latin *salarium*.

+ Salt used for pickling is not iodized because the iodine can darken the pickling vegetables and other foodstuffs. The effect is harmless, but aesthetically unappealing.

+ Some countries enhance salt with potassium fluoride to enhance dental health.

+ *Fleur de sel* (French) or *flor de sal* (Portuguese) means "flower of salt". It is collected in coastal towns of France, Portugal, Spain to high quality standards. Because of its relative scarcity and labour intensive production, it is considered an artisanal product, which its cost reflects.

# Outdoor Cleaning

## FIRE UP THE BBQ AND ENJOY A GREEN OUTDOOR SPACE

**FOR THOSE LESS** inclined to get their hands dirty in the soil but who still enjoy the outdoors, here's some tips and tricks for keeping your barbeque spick and span, making sure it's ready for that next cook out.

There's also plenty of advice on maintaining outdoor furniture and keeping it looking as good as the day it was bought, keeping the insects away and treating those pesky mosquito bites, and some natural flea treatments for man's best friend.

# Mosquito Repellent

One of the many problems with the commercial sprays for killing mosquitoes is not only their price but the chemicals we are spraying around the house to add to the cocktail of others chemicals.

▶ Fill a spray bottle with a cheap mouth wash, the el-cheapo from a discount store is perfect. Spray around the doors, windows, the verandah floor or lawn (if you are eating outside), on the chair you are sitting on, in the dog house and anywhere the little blighters are lurking. It will last a few days and give the air a fresh smell. The cost is only a fraction of the commercial chemical sprays and it's safer for you and the environment.

# To relieve the itch of bites

When you are bitten by a mosquito only a very small amount of the anti-coagulant chemical (venom) is injected and sits on the top of the bite near the surface of your skin. If you scratch the top of the bite, so that it bleeds, the venom flows out with the blood as the bite bleeds.

▶ If you would prefer not to scratch, dab the spot with some of the mouth wash you have been using as a repellent and the itch will disappear almost immediately.

▶ The degree of itch caused by a mosquito can depend largely on who and what her last victim was, and because a small amount of the previous victim's blood may flow into you as the mosquito sticks her proboscis in through your skin you can sometimes end up with a particularly itchy bite.

▶ If you do experience a very irritating bite try using a mouth wash designed for use when you have a sore throat rather than just the ordinary mint style mouth wash. The mouth wash for sore throats contains a mild anaesthetic that will numb the bite instantly.

▶ Alternatively saltwater or a poultice of salt and olive oil will help relive the itch.

▶ Because mosquitoes can carry disease it's best to avoid being bitten and if bitten attend to the bite as soon as possible.

# Stings from Sea Critters

If you're off to the beach take some meat tenderiser along, the enzymes in the meat tenderiser is a great treatment to relieve stings from jellyfish. Vodka has the same effect so if your day out includes a picnic with a vodka chaser you're doubly protected from the pain of jellyfish stings.

## Bee Stings

Bee stings hurt like hell, more so for the bee because they die as a result of their overenthusiastic attack on your flesh. As soon as you have been bitten cover the area with a generous amount of salt, it will help reduce the pain and swelling. Obviously if you are allergic to bee stings then you'll need urgent medical attention, you don't want to end up in the same state as the bee that stung you!

# ANTS

Ants have an amazing and highly developed community culture and they're fascinating to watch but they are also pesky little things if they've decided to move in with you.

Some simple ways to keep them out of the areas where they're determined to go is to draw a chalk line as a barrier, or lay down a salt line. Ants hate walking on both and you'll be ant free.

## Spiders

For those who are terrified of spiders nothing allays the fear of putting a foot into a spider infested boot. Keep the little blighters out by slipping an old stocking over the top of your boots when they're not in use. Make sure you use stockings free from holes and ones that are a nice snug fit.

The same method can be used for shoes left outside for occasional wear, slip them inside stockings and tie the end.

You'll be able to slip you feet into your boots or shoes knowing that there are no nasty little surprises waiting for you.

# To get rid of fleas

Flea bites are particularly annoying and you have to feel sorry for the dogs and cats of this world that are infested with fleas. Before fleas become a problem for us they go through many changes, four in fact; egg, larva, pupa and adult. The little black fleas you see, often referred to as ground or sand fleas, are the newly hatched adult flea. They have hatched, unfed, hungry and aggressive. They'll change colour and lighten once they have had their first fill of blood.

▶ Commercial pest treatments are obviously one way but quite often you'll need to have them come back again and again, it can be expensive and if you are trying to go more natural try the simple salt method.

▶ Sprinkle salt over the floors, leave overnight then vacuum. Salt absorbs moisture so it's not a good idea to leave the salt too long before vacuuming because it becomes moist and it's harder to vacuum up. This salt method is effective on any type of flooring and works by dehydrating the fleas. If you have a particularly bad infestation you can actually see them start to become very agitated and jump around.

▶ After you have vacuumed, empty the contents of your vacuum into a plastic bag, tie the top and dispose of in the outside bin. You may need to repeat the process once or twice. If you see a few of the little black fleas you know another lot have hatched and it's time to dispatch them with the salt treatment.

## Fido the host

A friend of mind recently tried bathing her dog in salt water after his weekly wash, leaving the solution on him for a while before rinsing him clean. She watched in fascination as the fleas began to abandon Mother-Ship Fido, leaping onto the ground only to die in the salt she had sprinkled around the wash tub. This is a cheap, effective, chemical free and inexpensive solution.

▶ However we don't suggest this for fleas on a cat, we doubt they would appreciate the lingering salty taste which would surely be a deterrent to feline personal hygiene.

## Lime and fleas

If you have fleas in the yard the old, and effective, method is to sprinkle lime around the house. This works in the same way as the salt trick and it was by sheer accident (and after long and protracted research) that we discovered lime can negate the effects of commercial pest treatments. We just throw this in to save you from the same learning curve we went through.

# FROST FREE WINDSHIELD CLEANER

Salt reduces the freezing point of water and was used in early versions of refrigeration in 'ice rooms', salt is used to keep highways safe after snow falls and we can use this principle to keep our windows and windshields frost free.

**Car windshield:** Put some salt in a cloth bag, wet the windshield then wipe it over with the salt bag. It will stop your windshield frosting up in the mornings.

**Household windows:** You can make the windows in your house frost free by wiping them with a solution of salt water. Alternatively mix vinegar and water in a ratio of 3:1 and spray on the glass as needed.

## To remove dead bugs from your car

You need to get rid of dead bugs from your car as soon as possible as their guts release acids that will eat into the car's finish. A small squirt of WD40 will loosen the bug so you can hose it off easily. WD40 is a fish based product and will also remove tar and grime from your car.

# Bird Lice

If you keep birds or chickens you have probably been exposed to bird lice at some stage and anyone who has experienced the effects of bird lice in their home will confirm that these tiny little specs of destruction are the most frustrating things to get rid of.

▶ Bird lice are close relatives of the tick. They are non discriminatory and are quite happy feasting on both animals and humans. The most effective method to rid your home of bird lice is to have the house fumigated, an expensive solution but very effective. This may not suit everyone, in particular people who have allergies or react to chemicals. However there is a quick fix — borax.

▶ Sprinkle borax on carpets, leave for a couple of hours then vacuum. Empty the vacuum cleaner immediately using disposable bags and store the bag in the freezer for a few hours to make sure you have killed all the lice before throwing the bag into the outside bin.

▶ For other surfaces mix ½ cup of borax and 4 tablespoons of dishwashing liquid in a bucket of hot water and use to wipe floors, walls and benches.

▶ Lice crawl from the ceilings down the walls so it is important to move furniture and beds away from the walls then wash the walls with the borax solution starting at the top and working your way down.

▶ The lice won't stop at crawling over walls and floors; they'll enjoy your company too!

▶ To rid yourself of these unwanted guests add Epsom salts to your bath water, it will relieve the itch and the bath will drown the lice. A dash of tea-tree oil will help seal the deal.

# Outdoor Furniture and Workspaces

Wicker furniture has a tendency to dry out when always kept in the sun and when soaked too often by rain or washing. But sometimes you need more than a vacuum to get it clean. To clean very dirty wicker, make a solution of 100ml of wood oil soap and 3L of water. Gently wipe one section of furniture at a time with a wet cloth, using a toothbrush to get at tight spaces in between the weave. Rinse the furniture with a hose and wipe it dry. Allow it to dry completely for 24-48 hours.

White wicker tends to yellow with age. To fight the effects of aging, before you store your furniture away for the season, scrub it down with a stiff brush and a saltwater solution of 150g salt and 750ml water. Allow it to completely air dry, preferably in the sun, before storing.

▶ Sprinkle baking soda directly on canvas chairs and hammocks, shaking off the excess, before storing.

▶ To get another summer's use out of old, weather-beaten lawn furniture, spruce it up with a baking soda wash. Wipe down all the surfaces with a solution of 50g of baking soda and 1L of water and rinse clean with fresh water.

▶ To combat motor oil stains in the driveway or sunbathing oil on the deck, pour baking soda liberally on the spot, letting the oil soak in for at least an hour before sweeping the soda away. For a stubborn stain on concrete, try lightly wetting the area before pouring the baking soda on top, let the soda sit for a few minutes before pouring a pot of boiling water on it. Scrub the stain and rinse. Repeat the process if necessary.

▶ Metal fasteners such as bolts, screws, nails, and hinges have a tendency to rust when left outside, exposed to the elements. To remove the rust, place objects in a container and cover with undiluted vinegar. Seal the container, shake it, and let the items soak overnight. The rust should be gone by morning. Make sure to dry the items to prevent corrosion.

▶ Old paintbrushes that have dried up can be revived if you've used them with water-based paint. (This won't work with dried-on oil-based paint.) Soak the brushes in a solution of 500ml of hot water, 30ml of vinegar and 60ml of baking soda. When dry, the bristles should be supple once again.

To remove rust, place objects in a container, and cover with undiluted vinegar. Shake it, and let the items soak overnight.

# TO **CLEAN** THE **BBQ**

Make a paste of equal parts bicarb soda and water. Apply with a wire brush then rinse with warm water and dry.

Alternatively, you can heat the grill to a high temperature and scrape it with a brass-bristled brush. While it is still hot, fold a paper towel into a tight pad and dip it in olive or vegetable oil. Hold the towel in between tongs and pass it over the grill grate by grate. Replace the paper towel once it becomes too dirty and repeat this process until the towel comes away clean. The grill should have a bright sheen when you're finished.

Occasionally fat from foods drips onto the coals of your fire and causes flare ups. Fight the urge to douse the flames with water, as this is counterproductive – it could send the flares shooting higher and reduce the temperature of the coals. Instead, keep a solution of 500ml of water and 5g baking soda in a spray bottle near your cooking area. Spraying the flames with the baking soda mixture will tame the fire without putting out the coals.

# Gardening

## STRENGTHEN YOUR **GREEN THUMB** AND GET YOUR **GARDEN BOOMING**

**FOR ALL GARDEN** enthusiasts these tips will help keep your private oasis free from all the nasty bugs and pests that can wreak havoc on a lovely garden bed of flowers or a crop of juicy vegetables, plus a few bonus tips on cleaning yourself up afterwards!

# FLOWERS AND PLANTS

Some general notes:

+ Lightly sprinkle baking soda on the soil surrounding tomato plants. Not only will it discourage pests from ravaging your plants, but it will produce sweeter tomatoes by lowering their acidity.
*Tip: Don't discard that box of soda you've been using to deodorise your fridge; it's still effective for use in your garden.*

+ If you grow your tomatoes in a container garden, work 5-10ml of baking soda into the soil when you plant your seedlings for the same sweet effect.

+ Occasionally dust a light sprinkle of baking soda around your plant and flower beds to discourage rabbits from having a snack.

+ If you have cracked concrete and sidewalks on your property, prevent grass and weeds from sprouting up by pouring baking soda on the ground and sweeping it into the cracked areas.

+ To clean clay flower pots without scratching them, avoid scrub brushes and soap. Instead, place a handful of salt on a clean, wet rag and scrub away. Rinse pots well with water.

+ Instead of commercially packaged solutions, add baking soda to the water in your cut flower vase to make the blooms last longer.

# GARDEN PEST CONTROL

Garden pests come in all shapes and sizes, from mould spores to weeds and poisonous plants. Here are some natural remedies to keep your plants healthy and your garden gorgeous.

## Cabbage Worm Fighter

Cruciferous vegetables such as broccoli, cauliflower, kale, bok choi, and cabbage (of course) are susceptible to a pest known as the cabbage worm, which is not a worm at all but the larvae of butterflies and moths that use such vegetables as host plants. In the morning or evening, when your plants are wet with dew, dust them with 125g of flour and 150g of salt.

## Aphid Fighter

Aphids (also known as plant lice, greenflies, blackflies, or whiteflies) are among the most destructive plant pests. Be a friend to lady bugs (or ladybirds) because they are a naturally occurring threat to aphids. But if you are not lucky enough to have lady bugs living in your garden, make your own safe pesticide. Combine the following ingredients and spray on any leaves where you see aphids. The lemon juice will render the plants inhospitable.

**15ml of lemon juice**
**15ml of baby shampoo**
**500ml of water**

# Black Spot Fungus/ Powdery Mildew Control

Roses can easily develop black spot fungus and mildew, which will eventually rid the plant of leaves and can even destroy the flowers if left unchecked. This effect not only makes your rose bushes unattractive, but makes it tough for them to survive the winter. Spray the following mixture on leaves once a week early in the morning to keep this nasty disease away.

**2L warm water
7g baking soda
2.5ml liquid detergent**

# Poison Ivy Killer

If you live in North America, it's likely that the mere notion of contacting poison ivy (which isn't ivy at all) makes you shudder and itch. To rid your lawn or wooded area of this rash-causing invader, add 1.5kg of salt to 3.5-4L of soapy water. Spray the leaves and stems of the plant to kill it. If it is covering a particularly large area, go ahead and pour the solution directly onto the plants. Be advised, this mixture will kill all sorts of plants, so take care not to wet anything you want to keep around.

# CLEANING YOUR HANDS

When you work outside, unless you wear gloves, your hands will get dirty and sticky. Here are a couple of effective hand washes for gardeners. Please take care not to use either method if you have cuts and scrapes on your hands or ragged cuticles around your fingernails, the effect will be painful.

## Pine Tar Remover

It's impossible not to get your hands sticky with pine tar when pruning hedges or hauling a Christmas tree in or out of the house. To remove the fresh-scented stickiness from your hands, forego the turpentine and opt for this natural alternative.

Place about 5g of salt in your hand, followed by a squirt of hand soap and about 5ml of lemon juice. Scrub your hands into a lather until clean. Rinse and follow up with your favourite hand cream as the lemon juice and salt can be abrasive.

## GARDENERS HAND WASH

Apply the pine tar remover (left), omitting the soap and simply using equal parts salt and lemon juice. Follow up with hand cream.

# METRIC CONVERSION

**FOR SOME OF** our readers, it might be helpful to refer to the following charts in order to covert the recipes in this book from metric measurements to standard (or customary) units, which are typically used in the United States.

Please note that metric "cup and spoon" measurements are only slightly larger than standard measurements, so they can be used virtually interchangeably with the metric measurements listed in the recipes. Often, you will find that both metric and standard measurements appear on liquid and dry measuring utensils.

## LIQUID AND DRY MEASURE EQUIVALENCIES *

| CUSTOMARY | METRIC |
| --- | --- |
| ¼ teaspoon | 1.25 ml |
| ½ teaspoon | 2.5 ml |
| 1 teaspoon | 5 ml |
| 1 tablespoon | 15 ml |
| 1 fluid ounce | 30ml |
| ¼ cup | 60ml |
| ⅓ cup | 80ml |
| ½ cup | 120ml |
| 1 cup | 240ml |
| 1 pint (2 cups) | 480ml |
| 1 quart (4 cups) | 960ml |
| 1 gallon | 3.84 litres |
| 1 quart = 32 ounces = approximately 1 litre (0.96 litres) | |

## LIQUID AND DRY MEASURE EQUIVALENCIES *

### BY WEIGHT

| | |
|---|---|
| 1 ounce | 28 grams |
| ¼ pound | 114 grams |
| 1 pound | 454 grams (0.45 kilograms) |
| 2.2 pounds | 1 kilogram (1,000 grams) |

## OVEN TEMPERATURE EQUIVALENCIES *

| DESCRIPTION | °F | °C |
|---|---|---|
| Cool | 200 | 90 |
| Very Low | 250 | 120 |
| Low | 300-325 | 150-160 |
| Medium Low | 325-350 | 160-180 |
| Medium | 350-375 | 180-190 |
| Medium High | 375-400 | 190-200 |
| Hot | 400-450 | 200-230 |
| Very Hot | 450-500 | 230-260 |

*All equivalencies are approximate and are provided by the United States National Institute of Standards and Technology (NIST), US Department of Commerce.

Metric "cup and spoon" measurements are only slightly larger than standard measurements

## CONVERTING FROM METRIC UNITS TO US CUSTOMARY UNITS **

| WHEN YOU KNOW | MULTIPLY BY | TO FIND |
|---|---|---|
| **Mass** | | |
| grams (g) | 0.035 | ounces (oz) |
| kilograms (kg) | 2.2 | pounds (lb) |
| **Volume** | | |
| millilitres (ml) | 0.03 | fluid ounces (fl oz) |
| litres (L) | 2.1 | pints (pt) |
| litres (L) | 1.06 | quarts (qt) |
| litres (L) | 0.26 | gallons (gal) |
| **Temperature (exact conversion)** | | |
| °C (degrees Celsius) | multiply by 9/5, add 32 | °F (degrees Fahrenheit) |

| CONVERTING FROM US CUSTOMARY UNITS TO METRIC UNITS ** | | |
| --- | --- | --- |
| WHEN YOU KNOW | MULTIPLY BY | TO FIND |
| **Mass** | | |
| ounces (oz) | 28 | grams (g) |
| pounds (lb) | 0.45 | kilograms (kg) |
| **Volume** | | |
| fluid ounces (fl oz) | 30 | millilitres (ml) |
| pints (pt) | 0.47 | litres (L) |
| quarts (qt) | 0.95 | litres (L) |
| gallons (gal) | 3.8 | litres (L) |
| **Temperature (exact conversion)** | | |
| °F (degrees Fahrenheit) | subtract 32, multiply by 5/9 | °C (degrees Celsius) |

**All conversions are approximate except for Temperature, which is exact.

# INDEX

# INDEX

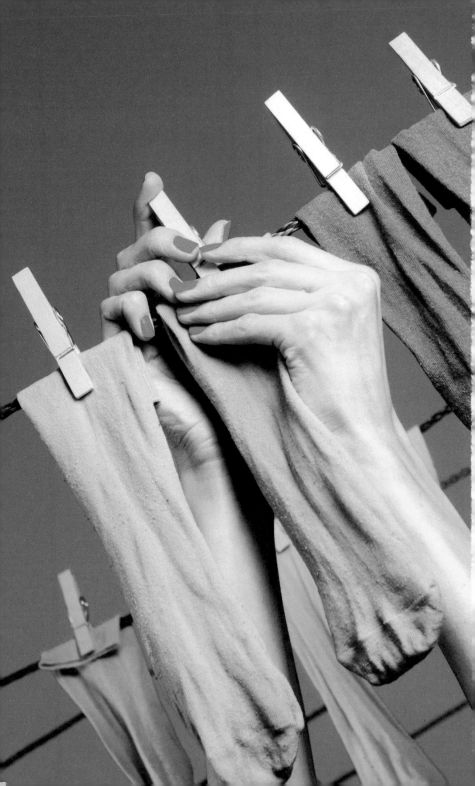